HE WAKENS ME

How to Pray When You Don't Know What to Pray

HE WAKENS ME

How to Pray When You Don't Know What to Pray

DR. WESLEY E. JOHNSON

REDEMPTION PRESS

Cover photo by Wes Johnson: Sunrise on Haleakala, Maui, Hawaii.

Published by Redemption Press, PO Box 427, Enumclaw, WA 98022
Toll Free (844) 2REDEEM (273-3336)

Redemption Press is honored to present this title in partnership with the author. The views expressed or implied in this work are those of the author. Redemption Press provides our imprint seal representing design excellence, creative content and high quality production.

Unless otherwise noted, all Scripture verses are from the New International Version

ISBN 13: 978-1-63232-765-9 (Print)
          978-1-63232-767-3 (ePub)
          978-1-63232-768-0 (Mobi)

Library of Congress Catalog Card Number: 2016934894

DEDICATION

To Terry and Archie: men whose passion for
God continues to impact lives long after
their departure to glory.

CONTENTS

PREFACE

Dear Reader,

Kathryn and I have always sought out companions on our spiritual journey. God has satisfied a great deal of this desire over the years in the many people who have come to hundreds of hours of seminars and retreats. I've included some of their comments here to help give you an understanding of what to expect from this book.

From long-time friend and small group partner, retired police detective Ken Thiessen, an elder at Madison Community Church, Everett:

> My first impression while reading the draft manuscript was, ahh . . . this is supposed to be a weekend retreat in a book! I found all the pieces: word of hope, being silent before the Lord, loving God with your heart, listening to and praying Scripture, breath prayer, praying our stories—the high and low points, soul friendship, and more. The *more* is what I found so compelling. Dr. Wes shares so much of himself, his life and experience with God calling, shaping and teaching him. Wes explained how he came to use these very same tools as God walked him through the valleys and mountaintops he experienced. He was describing relationship.

I have been asked from time to time, "How do I have a personal relationship with God?" This book clearly outlines how that relationship can begin, grow, and deepen. As Dr. Wes was sharing his own experience, I heard him saying, "I want you to have a growing, deepening relationship with your heavenly Father. Come join me."

Thankfully, through repeated exposure to what Dr. Wes was sharing, my desire for a deepening relationship with my Lord has taken root and grown. Learning to be silent before the Lord and listening for the instruction of the Holy Spirit as I read my Bible has been crucial to growing this relationship. I am cherishing my quiet moments with the Lord.

From the Stanglands, elementary through high school band directors and Awakenings Prayer Institute class members in 2014–2015:

I came to API in the fall tired, weary, empty. I've come out of API refreshed, filled with hope, and with a deep level of peace. Thank you both for allowing us to see your deep pain and also the joy that comes through working through it with God. —Robin Stangland

Thank you so much for the wonderful ministry that is API! This experience has really deepened my walk with the Lord and has brought the Word to life for me! I am also enjoying the friendship that is developing with you and the brothers and sisters at Bethel. Robin and I are excited about exploring what God has for us! And Kathryn, thank you so much for your wonderful music, worship, the food, and your friendship.—Dave Stangland

From Rev. Harald Gruber, former Pastor of Calvary Baptist Church, Washington, Iowa, regarding a customized API class at his church:

Your visit with us. . . was so meaningful and such a privilege. Reading the Word of God and looking at the details of the passages read made it come alive in new ways. Often we do not think about praying the Word of God, and being encouraged to do that makes it become relevant and real for personal intimacy with our Father. Taking time to focus on God's word of grace, mercy, and love for us makes it more real for our everyday life.

I have found that so many people are incredibly over busy with many things that are not essential in and for life. That keeps them from taking the time to spend with God and in his Word. Being able to be led away from that for some time and then seeing his reality is beyond anything we can find anywhere else in our busy life.

From Dr. Phil Templeton, director of counseling for the Cedar Park network of churches, Bothell, Washington, API participant and instructor:

On Breath Prayer:

What is a breath prayer?

It is two things joined together: a name for God and a prayer need. Maybe seven syllables, brief enough to be easily remembered and spoken in one breath. Deep enough to express my need and call out the name of the one who meets my need.

Early in my first year in Awakenings, I learned about breath prayer. One day in November, we were asked, "What do you need in your life right now?"

I answered, "Joy in Jesus," because I wanted to experience him in my life.

"Write a name for God that has to do with meeting your need."

I wrote, "Living Water."

Reading in the book of John, chapter 4, I saw Jesus talking with a woman at a well about living water that he alone could give. I thought about his water and what it could do for me. Water washes and cleans. It fills us and quenches our thirst. His water is life-giving and eternal. There is something deeply satisfying about Jesus' living water.

"Write a breath prayer," we were told.

So I wrote: "Living Water, wash me, fill me," because I continually need to be cleansed and filled by the one who loves me always and forever.

When our API session was done that day, I went home, and my wife traveled to Oregon to visit family loved ones there. I was quietly alone for the day with our dog and cat. That evening my brother called to tell me Mom had died. It was numbing, unexpected news . . . no one to talk with. . . . But I remembered the breath prayer and experienced the Lord in the dark hours before my family returned: "Living Water, wash me, fill me," I prayed at that time, asking the lover of my soul to hold me in his love when no one else was with me.

Finally, a few words of thanks.

So many have contributed to the making of this book. First, I want to thank my brilliant and dedicated wife, Kathryn, whose confident faith has fueled this project from beginning to end. Thank you, Sweetheart, for your stalwart support through dozens of retreats and seminars: for listening to seeking hearts, for leading worship, and for walking the pathways of prayer lifting this work to our Sovereign Lord and Abundant Provider. Thank you for those working vacations where you read over each chapter and contributed your thoughtful edits. Thank you for your faith, hope, and most of all, your resilient love.

And thank you to Theresa Schaudies, whose dedication to the institute has led to countless hours of creativity, critique, and constructive contribution. Thank you, Theresa, for reviewing lesson plans, producing top-quality materials, looking after a myriad of administrative details, providing leadership on retreats and seminars, and for gleaning the oh-so-helpful reflections of our participants for this book.

Thank you to the leaders of Bethel Baptist Church for valuing this training and discipleship ministry, and releasing me for untold hours of investment in the prayer life of God's people. Your passion for God and his people has contributed to the fulfillment of the Lord's calling in many lives.

Thank you to all of our API participants over the years, from the members of Bethel and other churches, to students at Bakke Graduate University, to counselors, pastors, missionaries, and others seeking to deepen their life of prayer. Your fellowship has enriched our lives as we have imparted to you the treasures of reflective prayer.

And to our readers: I pray your experience with this book will open unparalleled blessings of intimacy with our victorious warrior God.

In his peace,

Dr. Wes Johnson

FOREWORD

My comfort in my suffering is this: your promise
preserves my life.

—Ps. 119:50

A t different points in this book, you will learn about the story
of Jeremy Johnson. I am Greg, Jeremy's younger brother. The
author of this book is my uncle, and I can personally attest to the
value and power of lectio divina and breath prayer, to which my
uncle introduced me many years ago. I would like to share with
you how God answered my prayer to preserve my life and launch
me on a glorious course.

For three years (2005–2008), my family journeyed with Jeremy
through the valley of the shadow of death as he faced the formidable
foe of brain cancer. In September of 2008 at the age of twenty-seven,
Jeremy's health took a turn for the worse; the cancer metastasized
through his cerebral spinal fluid and into his spine. Three months
later, on December 13, the day of the first snowfall, Jeremy breathed
his final breath surrounded by family and intimate friends. Jeremy
went to be with Jesus.

My brother's death seemed to trigger a series of major losses in my
life. Five days after Jeremy died, one of my uncles on my mother's side

died. Not long after that my car broke down, and it was beyond repair. Then my family lost our home—the home Jeremy died in—and we were forced to move out. I hardly had a chance to say goodbye to the place, which had been a fortress of comfort for me, a refuge for my family, and a bastion of care for my brother.

While my brother was dying, I was falling in love with a beautiful young woman I had met at Seattle Pacific University. After Jeremy passed, I asked Rose Langer to be my wife on New Year's Eve. After being engaged for five months, the Lord counseled us to make a hard but good decision, and we ended our engagement. I vividly remember feeling like everything I had and loved was being taken away from me.

In the midst of the whirlwind of losses, I began desperately to cry out to God. I wrote voluminously in my journal every agony, every emotion, and every grief-swelled prayer that thrust me towards the comfort of Christ. But one simple prayer emerged from my grieving heart: *Preserve me!*

There were several Scriptures through which God ministered to me in those days: Psalm 119:50; Proverbs 3 and 4; and Hebrews 12:1–13, just to name a few. But for the sake of testifying to the value and power of lectio divina and breath prayer, let me share with you Psalm 119:50. It reads, "My comfort in my suffering is this: your promise preserves my life." So, my prayer became: *Preserve me!* Through this small prayer, I was able to communicate to God my great suffering, my deep need for comfort, and my desperate plea for him to save me.

The name of God I attached to this prayer was Good Shepherd. But I did not need to speak his name every time I prayed; I knew to whom I was crying out. He was the only one I could turn to for hope, for salvation, for preservation. Everything else was falling apart. I needed someone to hold me and to hold me together. I was afraid that I was going to die, that my grief would utterly consume me. And that is the very moment that God drew near to me as a loving Father, called me his beloved son, and said that he delighted in me.

Hearing those words was a soothing balm to my broken, torn-up heart. He knew that I needed the comfort of an intimate friend, of a strong yet gentle and compassionate father figure. So, my prayer shifted to, *Father, preserve my life.* And oh, he did. I discovered that in the deepest of pain, in the pitch-black darkness of bereavement, God was there, and he loved me. My Father loved me. Because of his great love, I was not consumed by my grief (Lam. 3:22). His love was a light in the darkness; he gave me hope beyond my despair. He reassured me with precious promises that he was with me, and that he always would be. I was comforted beyond words in the very crucible of affliction.

I was in a very vulnerable state in those desolate days, and my loving Father had compassion on me. As he continued to whisper his love and pleasure over me, he also provided much-needed financial aid through a generous brother at church. I was also greatly in need of a job, and in March 2009, he led me to work at Jamba Juice, which was a perfect fit at that time in my life. The money I earned there helped me to faithfully pay off student loans. What is more, another generous gift from a friend allowed me to take a basic chaplaincy training course at my church. During that course, a light shone in the darkness: the Holy Spirit filled me with the fresh and exciting vision of becoming a healthcare chaplain. God was intimately concerned with my life, and his answers to my prayer were flowing like a steady stream.

There is so much more I could say about those days, so many more testimonies of God's faithful, steady, comforting presence abiding so closely with me in my great grief. But what I want you to take away is to be real with God. Don't hold anything back. Open up your heart to him, and let him love you. It could be that you are experiencing immense suffering right now. Don't shut God out. I promise you, God hears your desperate cry, and he will come to your rescue. He will supply your deepest need. And then you will know, then it will be revealed to you, deep in your heart, right down to the depths of your soul, how much God loves you. Plant yourself firmly in the Word of God and in prayer, and you will witness him do marvelous things.

By the way, fourteen months after Rose and I took off the engagement ring, I proposed to her a second time, and she said yes. After a short engagement, we were happily married in Edmonds, Washington on October 10, 2010 (and we still are!). Then we packed up, moved to Colorado, and I pursued God's calling to become a healthcare chaplain by earning an MDiv chaplaincy degree from Denver Seminary after more than three years of study. Today I am serving as a chaplain in a hospital in Denver. Praise God from whom all blessings flow! Praise him whose love is unfailing! Praise God who preserves us in the midst of our pain and causes all things to work together for the good of those who love him (Rom. 8:28–29).

—Greg Johnson, MDiv

INTRODUCTION

"What do you need most from God at this season of your life?" That question penetrated my soul as it fell from the lips of a wise spiritual mentor. I had been speaking of the grief in my heart due to the loss of two of my closest friends. Each had contracted aggressive, untreatable cancers and died within eight months of one another. I had a sense in my soul of lonely isolation. I felt as though I were in exile from God, unable to sense his sustaining presence. That place where intimacy with God had once flourished had become a parched, spiritual desert. As I pondered the question, the answer rose from that isolated place deep inside. "I just want God to notice me!"

Of course I was aware that the omniscient God of our salvation knew exactly where I was, and his eye was upon me day and night. Yet my soul felt as if I had been cast out of the camp of the Lord. I needed the assurance that God had a plan to restore me from this place of grief.

Then my mentor asked another penetrating question: "What name of God tells you that he excels at meeting that kind of need?" The name leapt to my mind—Jehovah Jireh, the Lord who sees and therefore supplies. My director then said, "Now put God's name together with your need. What then would be the prayer of your heart?"

A simple, direct prayer formed within my soul, "Jehovah Jireh, look upon me—God who sees and supplies, just notice where I am. Lead me from this place of desolation into the place of your provision."

My director suggested I shorten the prayer to the most essential words and carry it with me throughout the day. That way I could pray it when I woke up, pray it on the commute, and pray it as I went about my daily chores. My prayer became, "Jehovah Jireh, look upon me."

The theme of exile in my short prayer led me to the biblical story of Hagar and her son Ishmael. In Genesis 21, this mother and son had been cast out of the camp of Abraham. They wandered in a desert, grieving and despairing of life. But then the Lord met them; he showed Hagar a well of water. He spoke promises of provision and of a future and a hope.

As I prayed my simple Jehovah Jireh prayer over the next several weeks and meditated on the Hagar story, a sweet healing began taking place. Then on retreat, the well of God's presence flowed fresh into the desert of my soul. At last I was able to tell God I was sorry for being angry with him at taking my dear friends home to be with him.

In short, I woke up to God's healing presence. My grief gave way to worship. My confusion gave way to the awareness of God's greater purpose—and best of all, I gained a refreshing sense of his presence healing and directing my life. Over the coming weeks and months, I began to form new breath prayers based upon the compelling needs I was facing in life and matching them to passages of Scripture.

Using this simple prayer pattern, I began to look back over the story of my life. As I pondered and prayed, I could see God's presence and purpose even in those moments when I had wondered if he was still at work. As I shared what I was learning with an experienced spiritual mentor, the awakening deepened.

Thus began a journey of restoration that has spread to many people. I began to teach this simple way of prayer to others. At retreats and seminars, in sermons, small groups and one-on-one, I began to share what I was experiencing. From pastors, counselors, and missionaries, to recovering addicts and the clinically depressed, this simple prayer pattern has assisted many to awaken to the presence and purpose of God in their lives and to pass the treasure on to others.

Here is what some of them are saying about Awakenings Prayer:

"It takes you deep into what God is doing through his word in your life. I found as I repeated the readings the text would come alive to my heart. It truly demonstrated it as a living Word active to my heart and deep needs."—a pastor

"I could finally hear the voice of my Lord. Wonderful!"—a lay leader who had taught Sunday school for over thirty years.

"At first I didn't think delving into the past and identifying past needs would have any value. As I did it, I found God's work in my life to overwhelm me again and again. . . . It was so rich and nurturing, even though it touched on some painful memories."—a pastor

"Breath prayer became the power of God breathing his character into the area of deepest need—this is powerful and transforming on the spot, in the moment. Breath prayer gives God the glory and the responsibility to make it so."—inner city Los Angeles youth worker and intercessory prayer leader

Now I want to open the way for you to discover your own deeper awakening to the presence and purpose of God in your life. What is Awakenings Prayer? Awakenings Prayer is a devotional journey into the heart of Jesus. It is listening, and it is obeying. It is enjoying, and it is sorrowing. It is climbing with God into the heights, and it is descending with Him into the depths. All along the way, it is companionship with our Sovereign Lord through the journey of life. Isaiah described in prophetic detail the life-giving connection Jesus had with his Father that led him on the journey of ultimate devotion:

The Sovereign LORD has given me a well-instructed tongue,
to know the word that sustains the weary.
He wakens me morning by morning,
wakens my ear to listen like one being instructed.

The Sovereign LORD has opened my ears;
I have not been rebellious,
I have not turned away.

—Isa. 50:4-5

The prophet portrays the Lord Jesus waking each morning to the voice of the Father. Because the Son is listening and the Father is speaking, Jesus has an unbroken awareness of the Father's presence and purpose. Because he hears the Father's voice through the triumphs and challenges of his earthly ministry, he has courage to endure even the suffering of the cross. He descends to the depths and rises to new heights through the power of the Father. Thus Jesus becomes the pioneer of a new way, the pacesetter for all who follow in the way of Christ:

Therefore, since we are surrounded by such a great cloud of witnesses, let us throw off everything that hinders and the sin that so easily entangles. And let us run with perseverance the race marked out for us, fixing our eyes on Jesus, the pioneer and perfecter of faith. For the joy set before him he endured the cross, scorning its shame, and sat down at the right hand of the throne of God. Consider him who endured such opposition from sinners, so that you will not grow weary and lose heart.

—Heb. 12:1–3

The apostle Paul speaks powerfully about the connection between the low points and high points of his life journey and the sufferings and exaltation of Jesus:

I want to know Christ—yes, to know the power of his resurrection and participation in his sufferings, becoming like him in his death, and so, somehow, attaining to the resurrection from the dead.

—Phil. 3:10–11

It is Paul's passion to be so identified with the risen Christ that even the lowest moments of his life may be experienced in partnership with Jesus. Paul is showing us that in all of life's sufferings and exaltations, we may experience the profound presence and guidance of the living God. Like Paul, we who seek to follow Jesus through the highs and lows of this life must gain the sense that we are somehow joined with Jesus, participating in the life of God. As Peter put it:

> Through these he has given us his very great and precious promises, so that through them you may participate in the divine nature, having escaped the corruption in the world caused by evil desires.
>
> —2 Peter 1:4

But how may we do so?

We need to hear what the Lord is saying to us in our triumphs, in our conscience, and in our tragedies. We need to cultivate a listening heart. As C. S. Lewis has said: "God whispers to us in our pleasures, speaks in our conscience, but shouts in our pains: it is his Megaphone to rouse a deaf world."[1]

Did you notice how Lewis describes the ways God speaks? He whispers in pleasure, he shouts in pain, and he speaks through conscience—that inner voice of the soul that is intended to align us with the moral character of God. Paul wrote of how a good conscience is an essential part of Christian obedience: "The goal of this command is love, which comes from a pure heart and a good conscience and a sincere faith" (1 Tim. 1:5). But our consciences can be horribly twisted. Our pleasures can become vices that destroy. Our pains can bury us in depression. All of these need to be transformed. For this we need the abiding grace of God's manifest presence.

Before he met Christ on the Damascus road, Paul believed that he was doing God a favor by imprisoning and putting to death the followers of Jesus. But God radically redirected Paul's mistaken conviction when the risen Christ revealed himself in a blinding light. In the most overpowering moment of Paul's life, he gained a radical new source of pleasure. He was given a new moral center—the person of Jesus himself—and he gained the overcoming power of God for his pain. Now everything was centered on Jesus.

And Paul's life journey became a participation in the divine nature, a partnership with God in Christ.

Through immersing ourselves in the gracious revelation of God in Scripture, we too may experience a moral reformation. God himself becomes our chief pleasure. He equips our conscience to perceive what for us is the surprising goodness of his will and to gain holy pleasures beyond what we had ever dreamed possible. He comforts and instructs us in our pain. Paul wrote of this moral transformation:

> Do not conform to the pattern of this world, but be transformed by the renewing of your mind. Then you will be able to test and approve what God's will is—his good, pleasing and perfect will.
> —Rom.12:2

As we encounter the Lord through the Awakenings devotional pattern, the Holy Spirit amplifies the whisper of God in the pleasurable events of life; he re-forms our conscience to reflect the morality of Jesus; and he clarifies what the Father is so powerfully speaking to us in our pain.

In the Awakenings experience you will:

Awaken to your soul's deep need to connect with the Lord: "Cast all your anxiety on him because he cares for you" (1 Peter 5:7).

Awaken to moral transformation through meditation on God's inspired Word: "For the word of God is alive and active. Sharper than any double-edged sword, it penetrates even to dividing soul and spirit, joints and marrow; it judges the thoughts and attitudes of the heart" (Heb. 4:12).

Awaken to the character of God revealed in his divine names: "The name of the Lord is a fortified tower; the righteous run to it and are safe (Prov. 18:10).

Awaken to the place of yielding and rest: "I have stilled and quieted my soul like a weaned child with its mother; like a weaned child is my soul within me" (Ps. 131:2 NKJV).

Awaken to the presence and purpose of God in the story of your life: "He who began a good work in you will carry it on to completion" (Phil. 1:6). "He reached down from on high; he drew me out of deep waters" (Ps. 18:16). "I press on toward the goal to win the prize for which God has called me heavenward in Christ Jesus (Phil. 3:14).

It's time to wake up. Let's begin.

Meet Your Fellow Awakenings Participants

Throughout this book, we will be tracking with twelve individuals who have engaged in the API experience. It is our hope that their reflections will provide you with a sense of camaraderie as you make your own journey with the Lord.

> Ken is a retired police detective and an elder at Madison Community Church in Everett, Washington. He has been a small-group partner with Wes for many years and has come on retreat several times. A quiet man, Ken is not comfortable with what he imagines will be forced intimacy with perfect strangers. He is a participant in API with his wife, Karen.
>
> Karen is a soft-spoken nurturer who has struggled to consider her own needs. Her life took a turn when she was diagnosed with stage three melanoma. After a protracted battle, she is inexplicably cancer-free today. She looks with gratitude upon the goodness of God in her life and in the lives of her family and friends. She has been enriched by the API seminars and is eager to share this spiritual journey with her husband.
>
> Rick is a classic extrovert—he loves people and being in a room full of them. He and his wife, Carol, are applying what they learned in a dozen years of church-planting among the urban poor in Brazil to the inner city poverty of Portland, Oregon. Immersing themselves in reflective prayer has helped Rick and Carol navigate the uncertain waters of career transition.

Dave is a gifted musician and educator. He is also owner and director of the North End Jazz Camp in Snohomish County. He is articulate and outgoing. At the October seminar he wrote: "I'm excited about this! Looking forward to growing and for deeper meaning in my prayer life." He is attending API with his wife, Robin.

Robin is a musician, teacher, worship leader, and owns her own business teaching homeschool band as well as private music lessons. She has been involved in Bible study and memorization for years, but in API Robin has been learning how to interact with God's Word in a new way. She loves meeting and getting to know a diverse set of people and loves getting together with other believers and hearing what God is teaching them through his Word. After the October seminar she wrote, "I am right where God wants me to be. . . . I'm jumping into the process and excited to see what God is going to do."

Stan is a former homeschooler who takes his role as a father very seriously. He and his wife Cathi have two boys. Stan describes himself as a person who sometimes dreads the group experience yet finds it fruitful. Stan is deeply interested in the Jewish roots of Christianity. He is studying Hebrew and is anticipating a work/study trip to Israel where he will volunteer with the Israeli government.

Marlee has a heart for women and welcomes opportunities to coach those who have been broken by life to experience who they are in Christ. God has given her an eye for beauty and a way with words, which she expresses through photography and Spirit-led blogging.

Judith is a scientist by education with the soul of an artist and a poet. She came to Christ in the Jesus movement of the sixties and seventies. Disappointed with church, she is looking for what she describes as an authentic relationship with God in communion with others. She discovered API by searching the Internet for a prayer retreat.

Charles is frequently surprised by (and extremely grateful for) God's continued presence in his life. Sidelined by disability, his quick wit and quiet friendliness has served him well on the several retreats he has attended. He always comes away refreshed by new insights and the unexpected pleasure of relaxed fellowship with others.

Gretchen is a retired elementary school counselor with a keen sense of humanity's woundedness and subsequent need for Christ's healing love. She has nurtured close relationships and cares deeply for a circle of friends she met through a divorce care group many years ago. She volunteers for the National Association for the Mentally Ill as a workshop instructor.

Phil is a licensed counselor and the director of counseling services at a large church in the Seattle area. A teachable teacher, he became intrigued by the possibilities for contemplative prayer as a resource for both himself and for his ministry.

Linda is a servant leader who volunteers at a pregnancy resource center where she is able to combine her gifts of compassion and organization. She has at times struggled against expectations that others have of her public role as "Phil's wife," particularly at church.

CHAPTER 1

HOPE THAT GIVES LIFE

And hope does not disappoint us, because God has poured out his love into our hearts by the Holy Spirit whom he has given us.
—Rom. 5:5

As you have picked up this book, what hopes do you have for your connection with God? At each Awakenings retreat and seminar, we begin with that question. What do you hope for? What moved you to come on this event?

Imagine that we have just driven a couple of hours to a secluded retreat center. We've left the busy chores of home far behind. It's been just over an hour now since we sped away from the four lanes of the crowded interstate, and you feel the tension of the last several days dropping away. We've traveled over country roads through verdant farmland and have arrived at our retreat center nestled at the base of a small mountain covered with cedar trees. Springs flow from beneath the mountain, feeding a series of large pools surrounded by well-kept gardens. We've unpacked the car and found our rooms. Now we sit together with a dozen other people on comfortable chairs around a conference table in a spacious meeting room where large picture windows invite our gaze out to the greenery of the cedar trees. As you look around the room, you know several of the people, but there are some that you have not met. You wonder how the weekend is going to go.

A leader comes around with a choice of colorful felt pens and asks you to write your name on a tent card that will mark your place for the duration of the retreat. And you are asked to write one word or phrase that expresses your hope for this retreat.

Why did you come?

What are you hoping for?

What do you need from God at this point in your life?

You ponder this in silence for several minutes. You notice that the whole group is silent. Some people are looking out the windows. Others are sitting with eyes closed. Others are writing on their tent cards. You notice that the leaders are also writing their names and words of hope.

You settle into the silence and think, "What am I hoping for?"

You write your word: *peace*. You think, "I could sure use some peace. It's been so chaotic lately." You think back to the family issues you've been facing, the tensions of your work place, and your sense of missing God in recent weeks.

"Yes, Lord, peace. I could use some peace."

And since you have an artistic bent, you draw an azure sky above a green mountain with a blue stream flowing down. "That looks like peace," you think. And then you let your vision drift out the picture windows, and you wonder what is up on that little mountain.

The leader draws your attention back into the room as he asks each person to simply share their name, their word of hope, and if they feel comfortable, a bit about why they chose it. As you listen, you hear people describe their hopes.

One person's one word of hope is *rest*. She talks about the busy pace of her life.

"Sounds like what I need," you think.

Another writes *inspiration* in large blue letters. He describes how he has been keeping pace with the demands of life, but his soul could use some fresh energy.

And you think, "Yes, me too!" As you listen, you find yourself empathizing with the others at the table.

"*Present*: I hope to be fully present here on the retreat and not distracted by problems at work, or what's going on at home. I want to be attentive to what is being said, to stay in the here and now."

"Right on," you think. You breathe out a prayer, "Lord, help me pay attention to you while I am here."

"*Learn*—my word of hope is *learn*. I want to learn how to do contemplative prayer better, for the healing it can bring. I guess *healing* is a better word of hope for me."

"What I am hoping for is *community support*. I want to be heard and understood and to not be derailed by negative human emotions."

"*Wisdom*," another shares. "I want to go beyond learning and experiencing—as good as those might be—and move toward wisdom. I hope to gain something that lasts."

"What I am hoping for is *clarity*. I have some decisions to make, and I am unclear about where God wants me."

"*Breaking bonds*. I want freedom from things in the past that are still hurting me—things that happened a long time ago but they have affected my circumstances all these years."

"*Resurrection*. I've been focusing on the crucifixion, the dying to self. Now I want to see the promise of new life fulfilled."[2]

And then it's your turn. What do you say? How do you describe what you are hoping for? A few more speak after you, and then you hear the leader describe his hopes for the retreat. He says that he hopes for companionship—he wants brothers and sisters who will be companions with him on the journey of listening to God.

Then the session moves into a season of prayer. Several name their words of hope and lift them up to the Lord.

You think, "This is going to be an interesting weekend. I wonder how God will meet us in this place."

But meanwhile, I'm aware that most of you who picked up this book are not away on retreat. You are in your home, or on a break at work, or perhaps in a coffee shop. Maybe you are fortunate enough to be overlooking a beautiful beach, a flowing river, or a quiet field as you read.

But I am hoping that you will take a moment to pause and consider the question we started with at the beginning of this chapter: What do you hope for as you read this book? Take a few minutes to reflect. Write your word of hope and a short explanation. Then lift that word of hope up to the Lord.

Let me say at this point that one of my hopes for you as you read this book is that you will take your time and interact with it at the level of the heart. Yes, this is a book for the mind. Jesus wants us to love God with our minds. But it is also a book for the heart. Jesus calls us to love God with our heart: all of it! But we twenty-first century, Internet-driven, tech-savvy, media-saturated North Americans are distracted. Our attention span is diminishing, and we are drawn in many different directions. With constant opportunity to connect with virtually anyone across the world through our electronic devices, it's hard to know where our heart is these days. And to be able to direct all the affections of our heart toward God is, well, daunting! Think about the challenges we face: How do we capture our stray thoughts? How do we direct those thoughts toward God? How do we become aware of what we are feeling? How do we direct our feelings into a single stream of love for the Father?

This is the quest of the heart that longs for God. It's what we need the most: the awareness of his presence. But here's the good news: Scripture is full of stories of God reaching to us, showing us himself. God wants us to know that he is on a quest to capture our hearts. Moses was minding his own business when that bush caught fire. From that day on, this living God, this self-existent one, the great I AM, became central to everything Moses said and did. He talked with God as a man speaks with his friend, earning him the title, "friend of God!"

God finds us.

Saul of Tarsus was moving quickly toward Damascus to arrest, torture, and imprison the followers of this new Way of Jesus. But God stopped him in his tracks. He heard the voice of Jesus. He saw the light of God. And he saw nothing more until Ananias, that faithful disciple, came to restore his sight and speak to him of the purposes of Jesus.

God finds us.

With the author of Hebrews, we could say the same about "Gideon, Barak, Samson and Jephthah, about David and Samuel and the prophets, who through faith conquered kingdoms, administered justice, and gained what was promised; who shut the mouths of lions, quenched the fury of the flames, and escaped the edge of the sword; whose weakness was turned to strength; and who became powerful in battle and routed foreign armies" (Heb. 11:32–34).

It all begins when God finds us.

Our part is to let God captivate us.

My prayer is that God will use this book to deepen your awareness of his presence and purpose and stimulate a greater love for him at the core of your soul. And I pray that such love will compel you outward to engage God's radical purpose with those around you. The good news assures us that God will meet us in this quest.

Consider your time with this book as time on retreat. Make it a journey of your heart as well as of your mind. Set your pace more like a quiet walk on mountain trails than a hurried run down a city sidewalk. Take your time. Savor each step. Pause and watch the streams flow down. Ponder the waterfalls, rest by the quiet pools, and listen.

Now, about your quest: what is your hope for your time in this book? Take a moment to write it here:

Now lift up that hope to the Lord. Tell God about what you hope for, and put your positive expectation in his hands.

Scripture for meditation:

Of David.

In you, LORD my God,
I put my trust.
I trust in you;
do not let me be put to shame,
nor let my enemies triumph over me.
No one who hopes in you
will ever be put to shame,

but shame will come on those
who are treacherous without cause.
Show me your ways, LORD,
teach me your paths.
Guide me in your truth and teach me,
for you are God my Savior,
and my hope is in you all day long.

—Ps. 25:1–5

Now Moses was tending the flock of Jethro his father-in-law, the priest of Midian, and he led the flock to the far side of the wilderness and came to Horeb, the mountain of God. There the angel of the LORD appeared to him in flames of fire from within a bush. Moses saw that though the bush was on fire it did not burn up. So Moses thought, "I will go over and see this strange sight—why the bush does not burn up."

When the LORD saw that he had gone over to look, God called to him from within the bush, "Moses! Moses!"

And Moses said, "Here I am."

"Do not come any closer," God said. "Take off your sandals, for the place where you are standing is holy ground".

—Ex 3:1–5

API Participants Respond with a Word of Hope

Judith's words of hope were *activate* and *abiding*, which she reports were totally fulfilled. "Steady on. Feeling very good about friendships." Conversely, the words of fear were *deactivate* and *perseverating*. She said God addressed this fear very well. Having slept well, her focus was consistent right up until the very end.

At the first seminar of the year in October, Gretchen wrote on her nametag two words of hope for the year: *honest* and *light*. "The fact that Pastor Wes and Theresa are genuinely engaged and walking along side us is key. The room is filled with a relaxed, caring feeling."

Rick's word of hope was *connection*. "The audio and visual of the rushing waters that cleanses me with his blood will always give hope and encouragement." His fear was that he would be unable to stay connected. "I will always live with this fear. My prayer is to turn this fear into the fear of the Lord."

Ken's word of hope at the first retreat was *direction*. He wrote in the retreat evaluation, "God re-directed me—God and I needed to settle an issue regarding his love for me."

Karen's word of hope was *stillness*. Her hope was fulfilled. "[It was good] being away from the busyness of everything around me and being still. I had nothing else to do but be still."

Dave's word of hope at the first retreat was *healing*. "God gave me some wonderful examples of healing and restoration. I'm taking away meaningful verses and breath prayers."

At the October seminar, Marlee said of her word of hope: "I had no idea how this exercise would set up the day. Holy Spirit inspired word is taking me where I need to go." Her word of hope at the final retreat was *hammock time*. Her prayer request was, "That I practice hammock time faithfully in this season. I went into it a couple of times and slept deeply at night."

Charles' word of hope was *learn*. He said afterwards, "I was taught by the Lord." His words of fear were *rebellion/pride*. Of this he said, God granted him "a keystone long missing in my identity."

Robin had two words of hope on the retreat: *hope* and *healing*. "He has led me to at least be bold enough to pray and ask for healing. He showed me that children with healthy fathers run to ask and good fathers delight in giving."

Stan's word of hope at the first retreat was *clarity*, which he says was significantly fulfilled. "Even if, via advisors, all my plans should ultimately seem unwise and need to be replaced, I have gained some skills to put into practice."

Phil's word of hope was adventure. "I was encouraged that next steps in my life will be well lit (Ps. 119:105). His words of fear were *harm to my loved ones*. "Psalm 91 covered it wonderfully."

Linda's word of hope was *advance*. She wrote that God fulfilled this hope "One hundred percent. He is so good to keep growing me as I make myself available." Her words of fear were *revelation, opening up to God*. "He let me stay in a safe place; nothing scary happened. Joy!"

CHAPTER 2

SILENCE

"Be still, and know that I am God;
I will be exalted among the nations,
I will be exalted in the earth."
The LORD Almighty is with us;
the God of Jacob is our fortress.

—Ps. 46:10–11

The longest day of my fifteen-year-old life took place in a hay field the size of Montana—or so it seemed. I was a suburban kid, born and bred, and here I was driving a gray and red 1949 Ford tractor and towing a hay rake around a twenty-acre field that seemed as expansive as the Big Sky State. I was missing my top-40 radio station, and in 1972 there was no such thing as an iPod to bring me my favorite tunes. I was completely alone in that windswept field, and the silence over the roar of the tractor engine was driving me crazy!

I had come to work for my seventy-five-year-old grandfather on the farm where he and Grandma had raised my dad and his six siblings. They grew Finnish yellow potatoes, corn, beans, raspberries, and acres and acres of hay. Grandpa had been cultivating those fields for over fifty years. I had left behind my newfound fascination with rock and roll, a job cleaning an audio visual store (a teenager's paradise), and cruising with my older brother to a very active high school youth group. Now my world consisted of the steady throbbing of the ancient tractor motor, the slow turning of the great tires, and acres of faltering windrows left in my wake.

I sang every song I knew. Beatles. Beach Boys. Hymns. Choruses. I quoted every Bible verse I had ever learned. I prayed for as many people as I could think of. I'd gone through my entire repertoire, and it was only 10:30 in the morning. This silence was killing me!

How do you feel about silence?

Fifteen years later, the silence I had hated felt pretty good to me.

I was a busy pastor serving my first church in a logging and mill town on the Pacific Coast. Enjoying a day off, I visited my parents on the family farm. When my father retired early from a productive career in education and moved back to the farm to care for his widowed mother, I understood his devotion but questioned the wisdom of this radical change in lifestyle. For much of his career, he had served as the director of mathematics and science for the Seattle School District, developing curriculum and training teachers across the city. He and my mother were well-ensconced in their suburban church. But the last five years of Dad's career had been a tumult of budget cuts and personnel reductions which had spun him from job to job in a spiral of downward mobility. In the end, he was serving as a vice principal overseeing the misbehaviors of junior high students. The light had gone out of Dad's eyes.

Now I was a weary thirty-year-old sitting on a stump watching my sixty-year-old father drive his high performance tractor around a wind-swept field. His face was tanned, his eyes focused, his hair flying in the breeze, and he was smiling. I thought, "The old man has done pretty well for himself." The Lord had met him in the silence of those great fields and, as King David had written in Psalm 23, restored his soul.

Let me ask again: How do you feel about silence?

King David penned those marvelous Psalms from a place of deep quiet. Just what did he do all day when he was watching sheep in the wilderness? Yes, there was a lion and a bear to fight. But when the drama of those battles was done, it was the silence. The quiet.

The sound of the wind. The bleating of the sheep. Hours and hours of quiet watching.

It was in the place of quiet that God trained this young man to be a king.

> He chose David his servant
> and took him from the sheep pens;
> from tending the sheep he brought him
> to be the shepherd of his people Jacob,
> of Israel his inheritance.
> And David shepherded them with integrity of heart;
> with skillful hands he led them.
>
> —Ps. 78:70–72

So much of the Bible comes to us from a place of silence. Moses tended sheep in the desert for forty years. Hosea was a picker of figs. Solomon wrote of vineyards and meadows where he courted the woman of his dreams. The Holy Spirit moved Paul to write letters from the lonely isolation of a prison cell. Jesus spent his childhood and young adult years listening to the beat of Joseph's hammer, the rasp of his saw on wood. And then he spent forty days in the wilderness listening to the heart of his heavenly Father and doing battle with the enemy of our souls.

God trains us in silence.

Richard Foster tells of Ammonas, a disciple of Saint Anthony who wrote of the transformation that takes place in stillness: "I have shown you the power of silence, how thoroughly it heals. . . . Know that by silence the saints grew, that it was because of silence that the power of God dwelt in them, and because of silence the mysteries of God were shown to them."[3]

Ammonas shows us that this is a particular kind of silence. It is a silence that rises out of holiness. It is a silence that is given but also must be fought for. Just getting to the place where our souls are stilled and our wills are quieted is a battle in and of itself. It is a battle to be still and know that he is God. We are everything but still!

Being still is a not just a challenge for a sensory-deprived teenager, a weary educator, or an exhausted pastor. This is a battle for every human soul who seeks the way of Jesus. We need instruction in the art of silence, and Psalm 46 is a good place to begin our training. After all, it is a warfare Psalm, and we are at war. Notice how the Lord surrounds his people in a time of great turmoil:

> God is our refuge and strength,
> an ever-present help in trouble.
> Therefore we will not fear, though the earth give way
> and the mountains fall into the heart of the sea,
> though its waters roar and foam
> and the mountains quake with their surging.
>
> There is a river whose streams make glad the city of God,
> the holy place where the Most High dwells.
> God is within her, she will not fall;
> God will help her at break of day.
> Nations are in uproar, kingdoms fall;
> he lifts his voice, the earth melts.
>
> The LORD Almighty is with us;
> the God of Jacob is our fortress.
>
> Come and see what the LORD has done,
> the desolations he has brought on the earth.
> He makes wars cease
> to the ends of the earth.
> He breaks the bow and shatters the spear;
> he burns the shields with fire.
> He says, "Be still, and know that I am God;
> I will be exalted among the nations,
> I will be exalted in the earth."
>
> The LORD Almighty is with us;
> the God of Jacob is our fortress.

—Ps. 46:1–11

When we begin Psalm 46, we see that God surrounds his people. Even though everything is changing, God is a very present help. It is a time of trouble. The earth is giving way. Mountains are falling into a raging sea. The nations are in an uproar. But the city of God stands secure because Jerusalem is fortressed about by the Almighty. Instead of a spirit of fear, there flows an unexpected river of joy. The city is refreshed by a spring of gladness welling up from the presence of God. How can this be? The answer is found in the refrain: "The LORD Almighty is with us; the God of Jacob is our fortress" (vv. 7, 11).

When we are aware of God's presence, gladness flows from deep within. His presence protects like a walled city. From this place, we hear the voice of God, and the rage of nations is stilled. It is in this situation that we hear the wondrous command: "Be still and know that I am God" (v. 10). But did you notice the verse before it? "He makes wars cease to the ends of the earth. He breaks the bow and shatters the spear; he burns the shields with fire" (v. 9).

The warrior God has brought the tumult to a halt. He has disarmed the warriors who were resisting his purpose. Arrows have stopped their murderous flight. Spears lie in the dust. Shields lay smoldering. How did this happen?

Picture our warrior God on the battlefield, advancing against the raging horde. Bows are raised against him. A thousand arrows fly. In ancient warfare, the bow was the weapon with the longest reach. But now, the Lord God has rushed the archers and broken all their bows. Long range resistance to his presence has collapsed.

Next he seizes the spears from the hands of the strongmen. He breaks them across his armored knee. The warriors can no longer hurl their spears at their divine enemy. Midrange warfare has come to an end.

Now the Almighty is engaged at close quarters. He wields the sword of his truth against the upraised shields of his enemies and shatters them. The warriors stagger backward. They fall to the ground and find the boot of the Almighty pressing upon their heaving chests. They hear his thunderous voice utter this compelling command: "Be still, and know that I am God; I will be exalted among the nations, I will be exalted in the earth" (v. 10).

They had thought to exalt themselves against the purposes of the Lord. But now they are in the place of humiliation. They can do nothing but surrender.

I remember surrendering to silence as an older teen. It was not something I sought. Like the enemy warriors of Psalm 46, it was thrust upon me. Pat Hurley, our Campus Crusade leader, had taken a carload of us to Portland, Oregon, to speak at a training event for area teenagers. It was a long drive back to the Seattle area. The 1973 Ford station wagon was full of teenagers. Patrick was driving, and I was sitting in the middle of the front seat next to him. About an hour into our return journey, Patrick began to shush me. Whenever I started to say something, he would shut me down. Now I have to admit, I was something of a talker. Pat must have grown weary of the sound of my voice because he would not allow me to say a word. I struggled mightily, wondering why he was treating me in this way. I began to think about all the good that he had done in my life—all of the training he had provided and the personal mentoring he had done with me. I reasoned that Patrick had done me good and not harm and that he must have a purpose in not allowing me to speak. As I thought this through, my anger subsided. I yielded to my leader's request that I be still. It was a powerful learning experience. Why? Because I trusted the heart of my leader.

We have a heavenly leader who is waiting for us to be still. Learning to be quiet in his presence is essential for us if we are to grow to be like Jesus. If we are honest with ourselves, we come to the place of understanding that we are that enemy. When we seek our own exaltation, when we set ourselves up against the Father's authority, we are, as Paul has written, in a state of alienation against the Lord (Col. 1:21). Picture the disciples of Jesus arguing about who among them is the greatest. Listen to the striving of your own ego, seeking to advance your own sense of significance. Then stop and listen to the voice of the Lord. Listen from the place of surrender. Having stripped away the weapons of our resistance, hear what he is saying to us: Stop resisting me. Stop striving against my purpose. Listen for my command.

In Psalm 131, King David contrasted the pride of our striving egos with the quietness of a contented child:

A song of ascents, of David.

My heart is not proud, O Lord,
my eyes are not haughty;
I do not concern myself with great matters
Or things too wonderful for me.
But I have stilled and quieted my soul;
Like a weaned child with its mother,
Like a weaned child is my soul within me.
O Israel, put your hope in the Lord
Both now and forevermore.

—Psalm 131

King David presents his stilled and quieted soul to the Lord. He does not concern himself with those things that are outside of God's plan for him. Could it be that our addiction to noise and distraction is really a way of rebelling against the Lord? We cannot hear him because we do not want to hear him. We are like the archers of Psalm 46, fighting to protect our right to rule our own lives. We want to do things our own way. We are like those ancient spearmen, hurling our pointed barbs at God, pushing him away. It is we who have raised our shields against the Almighty. We need the Almighty to rush into our ranks, take away the weapons we use to willfully resist Him, and bring us to the place of quiet submission. This is one of God's foremost goals with us: getting us to lay down our resistance so that we can hear him and obey.

Early in my pastoral years, I complained to the Lord, "Why are you holding me down?" It seemed to me that the Lord was keeping me in a place of obscurity. I had this feeling that he was pressing me down in the mud. But then the Lord seemed to say, "It's me holding you down; is that all right?" I gained a vision of the mighty hand of God pressing me down, and I realized that this was a very good place to be. Learning to listen to God is a battle. It is through surrender that we gain victory.

On occasion, Kathryn and I have enjoyed devotions from Philip Newell's beautifully designed *Celtic Benediction, Morning and Evening Prayer.*[4] Each devotion begins with a Scripture and then moves forward with this invitation:

Silence.
Be still and aware of God's presence within and all around.

I recall lying upon our bed, having read this gracious invitation, seeking to be aware of Him. From time to time I felt a reverent and holy awe of the Christ within. Then I sensed a whisper of his presence in our room, the one who fills all in all. Silence became the window into the eternal. We entered in.

For our thirty-third wedding anniversary, Kathryn and I spent five days on the Oregon coast. During the long drive south, we never turned on the car radio or plugged in a music CD. We talked, and we were silent. We didn't plan it that way; it just happened. We brought movies to play in the evenings, but we never watched them. We didn't turn on the television. We read books. We talked. We wrote in our journals. Each day we walked on a different beach. We took lots of photos and viewed them on our laptop at the end of the day. Most evenings we played guitar and sang music together, Kathryn on her sweet twelve-string, I on my acoustic bass.

We reveled in the gift of undistracted silence.

Take some time now to be still. Seek to be aware of the presence of God. Use a line of Psalm 46, Psalm 131, or perhaps Philip Newell's gracious words of invitation to focus your attention. If unbidden thoughts rise up, offer them to the Lord. Let him take the thought, and then return to the silence. After your time has concluded, reflect in your journal about what it was like for you to be silent.

Some hints about entering in to silence:
- Turn off your cell phone, close your laptop, or turn off your iPad.

- Set down your pen, close your journal. Relax your hands. Draw a deep breath in, and let it out slowly. Close your eyes if you like.
- Tune your awareness onto the presence of the Lord.
- If there are distractions in the room, such as the ticking of a clock, the heater, or air conditioner coming on or turning off, notice them, but then move your attention back to the presence of the Lord.
- If new ideas come to you in the silence, resist the urge to take up your pen or open your laptop and write them down. If they are from the Lord, they will return.
- Be still with God.

Interact now with the following questions:

1. What is it like for you to be silent?
2. What was it like focusing on a line of scripture or Philip Newell's invitation "to be still and aware of God's presence within and all around"?
3. Did unbidden thoughts arise? What did you find yourself doing with them?
4. What other distractions arose? How did you deal with them?
5. How would you characterize what you have gained from this time of silence?

Now take some time to read over the testimonies of others. How does your experience of silence compare with the following comments?

"My favorite devotional practice in this retreat was the quiet time of introspection."

"The devotional practice I found most meaningful today was praying in silence. I just couldn't separate myself from being in his presence. The silence was golden."

"I still have trouble getting my head into it—my problem."

"I would have preferred more quiet time."

"Loved the silence. Good practice."

"Good time of great stillness—it's been a while since I got that still with God. I'm going back to it for sure!"

"Silence with lectio is the most personal time you can spend with God—and my hardest."

Consider what the following people experienced in their times of silence.

API Participants Respond

After the winter retreat Stan wrote that the most meaningful experience was "walking and silent reflection on signature verses."

At the very first seminar, Dave wrote of his initial encounter with silence while reflecting on Scripture: "Redirecting my thoughts when my mind wandered, I was really able to experience what the Holy Spirit had for me." At the end of the first academic year, on a scale of one to five with one meaning "I completely agree," Dave gave a one to the statement, "I have a much higher tolerance for silence than I did before."

Karen struggled with silence but was rewarded by it consistently. "It is great to start with silence," she said. At the first retreat she asked for prayer to "be able to turn things off—TV, radio, Internet, cell phone, people—and make time to be silent. I want it. I know it is what I need to do. When I do it, I feel more satisfied and ready for the day."

Marlee admitted on one seminar evaluation: "I talk too much and struggle to be a good listener and not interject." But during silence with breath prayer, Marlee reported: "I got some breakthrough insights from this prayer to use in my coaching."

About the silent time with just her journal and Psalm 139, Robin reported, "God showed me many things with verses 23–24." Reflecting on Richard Foster's book, *Sanctuary of the Soul*, she wrote, "Our attitudes can affect others, even when we are quiet, just by our spirit being in touch with God."

What Ken appreciated about being able to still his own thoughts is "that [he] could listen should God choose to speak. If all you do is talk to God, you miss out on what he has for you and getting to experience his love." And later he reflected, "Learning to be silent and listening to the instruction of the Holy Spirit as I read my Bible has been crucial to my growing relationship with the Lord. I am cherishing my quiet moments with him."

Charles said, "In private prayer—in Scripture reading—silence is essential to sense God's presence. Silent moments throughout the day let me return to rest in God."

At the end of the year Judith reported having a much higher tolerance for silence than before. However, sometimes it is still a struggle. In March during a period of silent reflection, she wrote: "I was having internal struggles focusing." At the end of the year, she reported real fruit from her times in silence: "Congruent with my growth in the discipline of silence has been a rekindling of a very deep creative fire."

Although Phil had practiced contemplative prayer before, he still gained a greater level of comfort with silence. He said he has, "learned to treasure the silence." He described the silent time spent praying during each seminar as, "entering in—a good activity to focus what we've done since the last meeting."

What Linda appreciated most on both retreats and seminars were the structured times of quiet retrospection. "A structured time with intent is so much less awkward than silence without direction."

Gretchen valued the times of silence because, she said, "It was good to be private." Of silent contemplation, she wrote, "I feel great peace, trust, and freedom because I learned ways to just plain focus on God. . . . We are with God by immersing all of our senses."

Early in the year, instead of feeling rejuvenated during the silent periods we call Refresh and Reflect, Rick said he felt like he was just catching up. However, four months later he wrote about this time that it was, "Always excellent!" He particularly enjoyed the silent time of reflecting on Psalm 139.

CHAPTER 3

LOVING GOD

"Love the Lord your God with all your heart and with all your
soul and with all your mind and with all your strength." The
second is this: "Love your neighbor as yourself." There is no
commandment greater than these.

—Mark 12:30–31

Now I would like to invite you to move into the experience of
loving God through the Scriptures. This is a way of loving and
listening to God with the heart.

We in the West have approached God and life principally
through the mind. We think, we reason, we read, we make judgments, we debate. We believe in the power of education to improve
life for us all. All of this is good. In fact, Jesus says that we must
love God with our mind—all of it! He wants us to really think about
life, and in doing so, to offer our minds up to him.

Dr. Philip Dow in his wonderful book, *Virtuous Minds:
Intellectual Character Development,*[5] describes God's quest to fashion
our moral character through the ways we think. Dow calls his
readers to love the truth through the seven habits of intellectual
courage, carefulness, tenacity, fair-mindedness, curiosity, honesty
and humility. These are traits that integrate the elements of Jesus'
great command to love God above all else and to love our neighbor

as ourselves. In his writing, Dow attributes characteristics normally associated with the heart to the life of the mind. He thus provides a powerful corrective to the Western habit of exalting the mind over the heart.

Let me illustrate. Many Christian seekers learn to approach God with the mind but struggle to interact with him at the level of the heart. They believe that if they can master the facts of faith, then they will learn to know God and grow in maturity. When they read Scripture, it is through the lens of reasoning. But rather than judging the Scripture, we need to allow the Scripture to judge us. We need to look at things from the inside out, not the outside in.

Here is what it looks like up close and personal. I was having a series of spiritual conversations with an intelligent, inquisitive spiritual seeker. He was a science student at the university, and he thrived on asking questions. We had some great times together. He would pepper me with questions about God and faith, and I would do my best to volley his shots back to him. Once I met a friend of his who was in his class study group. I asked her what it was like to study with him, and she talked about how many questions he asked. His questions moved the group to some great discussions. I knew then that he was a sincere seeker of truth.

One day in our spiritual discussion as he asked me question after question, I asked him something that pulled him up short. "What would it look like for you to love God with your mind?"

He looked at me as if I had two heads. "What do you mean?" he asked.

I said, "You have a magnificent mind. Your questions are deep. You think hard about things, and you really want to know the answers. But what would it look like if you decided to love God with your mind?" He pondered this for a while, and that was the end of our discussion that day. That same evening, he later told me, he went up to his room and surrendered his intellect to the Lord. It was the beginning of an exciting spiritual adventure for him as he became an ardent follower of Jesus.

You see, according to the Great Commandment, God has designed our minds to be the servant of love. Jesus said that the greatest commandment is that we must, "love the Lord our God with all our heart, all our soul, all our mind, and all our strength" (Mark 12:30). The critical thinking that we do, the questions we ask, the reasoning processes that we engage—all of this has been given to us by our Creator so that we may love him well.

But in the West, we have demoted love and made the mind preeminent. In fact, many people worship the intellect. Great minds have studied the sciences and decided that we do not need God. One of my college professors claimed that sociology was the answer to everything. He publicly mocked faith and exalted his own field of science. But when human beings reason and conclude that we know more than God knows, that our knowledge qualifies us to make judgments that exclude Him, we have left the realm of the great commandment. God gave us magnificent minds so that we might love a magnificent God in magnificent ways.

Here is another example. Richard Foster tells the story of Jim Smith, a brilliant graduate student who spent several frustrating days on a personal retreat. He was assigned by his retreat director to read and re-read Luke 1:26–38. In this passage the angel Gabriel announces to Mary that she would be mother to the Messiah. The passage concludes with Mary's compelling words, "'I am the Lord's servant,' Mary answered. 'May your word to me be fulfilled'" (v. 38). Jim Smith records how he spent the first day doing a critical analysis of the words of the text and getting some talking points for his next Christmas sermon. His mind was busy, but his heart was not engaged. He was restless, unfulfilled.

Later that day he met with his spiritual director who asked him, "Did you experience God in your reading?" I get the feeling that Jim looked at his spiritual director the way that my university student friend looked at me. So his spiritual director sent him back to ponder the passage with the instruction to not try so hard, but to simply let the passage speak to him from the heart of God. Through all the next morning, Smith's frustration only grew. For him the passage was lifeless—just facts on a page. The silence was deafening. But then at noon on the second day, he lifted up his sense of futility to the Lord, and everything shifted. Here's how Foster describes it:

As Jim sought to meditate further on the passage, he cried out in frustration. "I give up! You win!" . . . He slumped over the desk and began weeping. A short time later he picked up his Bible and glanced over the text once again. The words were familiar but somehow different. His mind and heart were supple. The opening words of Mary's response became his words: "Let it be to me . . . let it be to me." The words rang round and round in his head. Then God spoke. It was as if a window suddenly had been thrown open and God wanted to talk friend to friend. . . . .

The Spirit took Jim down deep into Mary's feelings, Mary's doubts, Mary's fears, Mary's incredible faith-filled response. It was, of course, a journey into Jim's feelings and fears and doubts, as the Spirit in healing love and gentle compassion touched the broken memories of his past.[6]

Jim Smith learned what it was to move from a mind-centered quest that seeks to somehow control a passage of Scripture to a heart-centered passion to commune with the living God.

Paul had this in mind when he wrote, "Knowledge puffs up while love builds up" (1 Cor. 8:1).

Our problem is that the intellect often becomes the master and pushes love to the side. Robert Mulholland in his brilliant book, *Shaped by the Word, The Power of Scripture in Spiritual Formation,* contrasts an informational approach to Scripture that is about a desire to know, and thus perhaps to control or manipulate the information in the Bible, as Jim Smith was attempting, with a formational approach to Scripture, which is about the "adventure, search, hunger, journey, quest, pilgrimage" toward Christ-likeness. Mulholland challenges believers to move away from the habit of over-thinking the Christian faith and move to the level of encounter with the "living, penetrating, transforming Word of God."[7]

I continue to deeply appreciate the seminary education I received as a young man. We learned to think the thoughts of the great theologians of the church. We learned to read Scripture in the original languages and analyze biblical texts using the tools of grammar and syntax. I recall one of my seminary professors underscoring the value of mastering the basic tools of language.

He asked: "Do you love truth my friend? Then do not despise grammar, for the sword of truth rests in the sheath of grammar."[8] But if all we do is, as Jim Smith said, "Arrive at an understanding of the meaning of the text,"[9] our hearts are left crying for more. Yes, we need to know the mind of God, but even more, we need to know his heart.

To grow in love for God, we must move from the dispassionate analysis of the mind to a warm response of the heart. We must move from analyzing language into a wrestling of love that requires strength of both mind and soul. Spiritual leaders should work hard, as Paul said, at the task of preaching and teaching (1 Tim. 5:17). Pastors and teachers should love God with their strength. They should be stimulated to use their minds to read the great authors and learn all they can from those around them. But the spiritual life is more than an intellectual pursuit. It is the realm of the heart; it is the work of the soul. Richard Foster comments on the transformational experience of meditating on Scripture: "In Meditative Prayer the Bible ceases to be a quotation dictionary and becomes instead 'wonderful words of life' that lead us to the Word of Life."[10]

The sons of Korah wrote of the passionate quest for God:

As the deer pants for streams of water,
so my soul pants for you, my God.
My soul thirsts for God, for the living God.
When can I go and meet with God?

—Ps. 42:1–2

There is a great deal more than intellect operating in this quest to know and love the Lord. Believing in God goes beyond the mind; it includes the heart, the soul and our very strength.

There is a very close relationship between believing in and knowing someone or something. The writer to the Hebrews teaches us that faith is a way of knowing, a way that involves more than our reasoning:

> By faith we understand that the universe was formed at God's command, so that what is seen was not made out of what was visible.
>
> —Heb. 11:3

Faith is a way of gaining profound understanding about the origin of the universe. Paul reminds us that in addition to faith, hope is also a way of knowing:

> Therefore, since we have been justified through faith, we have peace with God through our Lord Jesus Christ, through whom we have gained access by faith into this grace in which we now stand. And we boast in the hope of the glory of God.
>
> —Rom. 5:1–2

This kind of hope teaches us to have great confidence in the Lord, a confidence that grows as a response to God's amazing love:

> Not only so, but we also glory in our sufferings, because we know that suffering produces perseverance; perseverance, character; and character, hope. And hope does not put us to shame, because God's love has been poured out into our hearts through the Holy Spirit, who has been given to us.
>
> —Rom. 5:3–5

Additionally, there is a peace that surpasses the greatest ability of the mind:

> Do not be anxious about anything, but in every situation, by prayer and petition, with thanksgiving, present your requests to God. And the peace of God, *which transcends all understanding*, will guard your hearts and your minds in Christ Jesus.
>
> —Phil. 4:6–7 italics mine

This peace of God enfolds the intellect, puts the mind at ease, and brings the soul to rest in the goodness of the Lord.

But the greatest way of knowing is the knowledge that comes through love.

The unknown author of the great fourteenth century work of Middle English spirituality, *The Cloud of Unknowing*, speaks of the mystery of apprehending God by means of love. *The Cloud* states of God that, "By love he may be gotten and beholden: by thought never."[11] This is not to say that we cannot know true things about God. Spiritual thoughts and spiritual words give us spiritual truth (1 Cor. 2:13). But there are things about God that are simply beyond our understanding. As Romans 3:23 assures us, all aspects of our character will fall short of God's glory. This includes the way we think. God made this plain through the prophet Isaiah:

> As the heavens are higher than the earth,
> so are my ways higher than your ways
> and my thoughts than your thoughts.
>
> —Isa. 55:9

Some things about God are simply beyond us. No wonder the writer of *The Cloud* concluded: "To our intellect . . . he is evermore incomprehensible, but not to our love; therefore, it is through the heart, and not the intellect, that one is able to know God."[12] We are back to the psalmist and his panting soul, longing for God.

But think for a moment about the heart-rending story of Job. In his great suffering, Job requested an audience with God. He was looking for answers to the great question of why he was suffering so. But God never set Job's mind at ease by answering his questions. God never explained his actions to Job. These things were simply beyond Job's understanding, and as he yielded to God's sovereignty, he found great peace.

> Then Job replied to the LORD:
> I know that you can do all things;
> no purpose of yours can be thwarted.
> You asked, "Who is this that obscures my plans without knowledge?"
> *Surely I spoke of things I did not understand,*
> *things too wonderful for me to know.*
>
> —Job 42:1–3, emphasis mine

Though God chose to not let Job in on the reason for his suffering, he comes to be with Job, and in this presence, Job abandons his right to know the mysteries of God. When he does so, he finds healing:

You said, "Listen now, and I will speak;
I will question you,
and you shall answer me."
My ears had heard of you
but now my eyes have seen you.
Therefore I despise myself
and repent in dust and ashes".

—Job 42:4-6

Faced with the hiddenness of God, the writer of *The Cloud* speaks these words of marvelous hope: "Yet such is God's grace that the soul is made sufficient to the full to comprehend him by love."[13]

What we cannot grasp with our minds, we can apprehend with our hearts. Where the intellectual powers of the great theologians fall short, the Holy Spirit of God bridges the gap. We cannot capture God and analyze him like a science project. Instead, he has willed it that we should come to know him in a deep and personal way, the way that a child who grows into maturity comes to know, love, and trust a father of noble character. Paul spoke of this mature love that is able to press past the limits of simple reasoning. In 1 Corinthians 13, his great chapter on love, Paul compared our partial knowledge of God to that of a child who comes to greater knowledge as he grows to manhood:

When I was a child, I talked like a child, I thought like a child,
I reasoned like a child. When I became a man, I put the ways of
childhood behind me.

—1 Cor. 13:11

Paul is taking us back to those childhood memories of carefree dependence.

When my siblings and I were children, we would rely upon our parents for everything—including getting anywhere our bicycles could not carry us. Mom or Dad would drive us, and that was that.

My dad was a Ford man. When we rode in the family car, it was a Ford Fairlane, Falcon, or a Country Sedan station wagon. Thinking like a child meant that I never wondered how much the car cost or how much money it took to keep it running. What my brothers and sister and I wondered about was who was going to get a window seat and who would get stuck in the middle! But we knew that Dad would drive, Mom would sit up front beside him, and we kids would pile in the back seat and go to all kinds of amazing places. This is the simple knowledge of a child.

But Paul moves us past the years of carefree dependence into the years of maturity. When I was in my early twenties, my father gave me a classic 1966 Ford Mustang. Over the next eighteen years, I learned what the car was worth. I experienced the cost of a rebuilt engine, a new transmission, body repairs, and paint jobs. No longer was I reasoning as a child. I was thinking like a grown man, a fully responsible car owner. Then for his seventieth birthday, I gave the Mustang back to my father. I told him I wanted him to use it to take Mom out on dates and to drive it in parades. All I asked was that he would return the car to me on his ninetieth birthday. No longer did I reason like a child. As a mature adult I wanted to honor my father for his sacrificial love. It brought me great joy to be able to give him that car. Later I had a license surround made with the slogan, '66 Mustang, Like Father, Like Son. Generosity had come full circle. I had moved from depending on Dad as a child to honoring him, man to man, son to father. And the bond between us matured greatly. (My father kept the Mustang until his health declined in his mid-eighties. He returned the car to me before he died, and it continues to be a reminder of sacrificial, generous love.)

Dad and I had "apprehended one another by love." We had moved from intellectual affirmations about the value of classic Ford automobiles and how to drive from point A to point B. We had moved beyond the factual knowledge that we are father and son to the heart knowledge of being loved, treasured and respected. We had apprehended one another by love.

Paul speaks of this maturing love using the metaphor of a very imperfect mirror. Immature love is like trying to make sense of the world through a distorted glass. But when God's full expression of love comes, we will see everything clearly. We will know and be known completely:

> For now we see only a reflection as in a mirror; then we shall see face to face. Now I know in part; then I shall know fully, even as I am fully known. And now these three remain: faith, hope and love. But the greatest of these is love.
> —1 Cor. 13:12–13

The child grows up. The vision clears. Partial understanding gives way to profound intimacy. This is the knowledge that comes through love. Jesus spoke it plainly: the mind is the servant of love and not the master. When we move into the realm of such love, we find ourselves in deep communion with our triune God. Love is how God communes with us. It's not that he bypasses the mind; rather, he uses the gateway of the intellect to gain access to the deepest places in our spirit. Even when the mind fails, his communion with his beloved does not.

One of the most profoundly spiritual women I have known was my father's mother, Alvina Johnson. Along with her husband, Arvid, a hard-working farmer and logger, she raised seven children on a small farm in Skokomish Valley, Washington. She read the Scriptures, she prayed deeply, she gave generously, and she gained a profound grasp of what it was to live close to Jesus. She understood the ways of the Spirit working in the human soul, a wisdom that flowed from a life of faith, hope, and love. Tragically, however, in the closing years of my grandmother's life, she lost the use of her mind. She no longer recognized her loved ones. She wondered how the little people got inside the television at the foot of her bed. Like a simple child, she wore a bright ribbon in her hair and clutched a little doll. But one day, Karen, a young woman from the community came to see Grandma. She asked my Aunt Edith if Alvina could pray for her. Edith, a veteran missionary of forty years and a person powerful in prayer, replied that her mother no longer prayed for people; she didn't know anyone anymore. But Karen insisted, and finally Edith relented. Karen entered Grandma's sunlit room and simply folded her hands in the posture of prayer. What happened next moves us out of the realm of brain science and into the mystery of the Holy Spirit's presence in the human soul. A delighted look moved across Grandma's face. She folded her hands in prayer and enthusiastically said these words, "Dear Lord, please bless and keep this young woman as she travels by train to New Jersey. And help her tell her family all about you. Amen!" At this point, Edith made the familiar circular motion with her index finger up next to her temple, indicating that she believed her mother's words were simply crazy. But Karen, to Edith's astonishment and delight, was overcome with joy. Alvina had prayed exactly what Karen was about to do—travel by train to New Jersey with the hope of speaking to her family about Christ.[14]

What had happened? The Holy Spirit had moved past the brokenness of my grandmother's diseased brain and had spoken truth directly to her spirit. Her mind no longer worked, but her spirit that day served as a very able conduit of divinely directed prayer. The Spirit of God was communing with her spirit. Even in her extreme weakness, she was a part of the divine communion of love, bringing forward a living message that resulted in great delight. What a comfort! What a hope.

Paul writes eloquently about the limits of our minds. In Romans 8:26 and 27, he teaches that when we come to the end of our ability to know the will of God, the Spirit is indeed very active. We have high hopes, (v. 25), but we have no idea of how God is going to work things out (v. 28). We don't even know how to pray (v. 26). It is then that the Spirit communes with us in ways that move beyond logic.

> In the same way, the Spirit helps us in our weakness. We do not know what we ought to pray for, but the Spirit himself intercedes for us through wordless groans. And he who searches our hearts knows the mind of the Spirit, because the Spirit intercedes for God's people in accordance with the will of God.
>
> —Rom. 8:26–27

Just as my grandmother's mind had no capacity to know what to pray for (Karen had not spoken a word about her train trip), our minds also reach the limits of logic and understanding. How can we know the purpose of God Almighty? How can we discern the will of the Father? Like Job, we find that it is often beyond us—way beyond our capacity to know and understand. But we do not have to give up praying. In fact, it is at this point that our prayers can move us into great intimacy with the triune God. When we surrender to the Father who searches our hearts (v. 27), when we yield to the Spirit who prays in us (v. 27), and when we submit to the Son who prays for us (Rom. 8:34), we learn the wonder of being part of the divine prayer meeting!

When our twenty-four-year-old nephew Jeremy was diagnosed with an aggressive brain cancer, the news pierced us like a spear. During his three-year battle, we struggled with God. We asked, "Why him, Lord? Why us? Why must our family suffer like this?" I felt drawn to meditate on Romans 8:22–29. As I prayed over this passage, I noticed that we all are part of a fallen creation, and in this creation we groan. But I also noticed that the Holy Spirit groans with us. These reflections on Romans 8 led me to a greater acceptance of the fallenness of life. After all, who are we that we should be exempt from the ache that emanates from the heart of all creation?

As I meditated upon verse 27, I saw that while I did not know how to pray, nor did I know what God was going to do, the Father and the Spirit knew both. The Father was searching our hearts. He knew our longings and desires: a rich and full life for our beloved nephew. All the while, the Spirit was speaking his mind to the Father, and what he was praying for us was in line with the Father's will. This became a great comfort. We did not know the Lord's will, but we knew that he loved us.

So it became clear to us to pray something we knew was the Father's will. A singular prayer emerged: "Lamb of God, triumph in our suffering. All we want is your triumph in this. Get honor for your name, Lord Jesus. You who triumphed through death and resurrection, get your triumph through Jeremy's illness."

That prayer called us to a place of profound yielding. It called us out of trying to make deals with God. It called us away from wondering if we had the kind of faith that could move mountains and bring healing to our nephew. It called us back to a core value that resonates with the passion of our lives: Jesus, be honored. Get your triumph. It's not about us. It's about you. It's about people seeing how magnificent you are. It was about loving God, especially when we could not understand.

What questions do you have for God that you just don't see any answers for? When you reach the limits of your understanding, what is your response? What would it look like for you to love God with your mind?

Take some time to meditate on Romans 8:22–39. As you notice the groan and ache of living within this fallen creation, notice also the rich communion of the Father, Spirit, and Son. What is it like for you to ache with the fallen creation? What is it like for you to commune with the triune God in the new creation? Take time to meditate on the conversational flow between the Father, the Son, and the Spirit. Consider what it would be like to listen in to the triune communion.

Conclude your meditations by reflecting on God's love:

> For I am convinced that neither death nor life, neither angels nor demons, neither the present nor the future, nor any powers, neither height nor depth, nor anything else in all creation, will be able to separate us from the love of God that is in Christ Jesus our Lord.
>
> —Rom. 8:38–39

Take time now to pray this prayer from Richard Foster: "O wine of my heart, intoxicate me with your love. For Jesus' sake. –Amen."[15]

API Participants Respond

Notice that some comments come from the workings of a curious and fine mind while others come straight from the heart; one is more analytical, the other more emotion based. As you read, ask yourself if you tend to love God more deeply with your heart or with your mind.

At the second retreat, Rick commented on a film we watched about how one man's heart was healed by a unique encounter with his past and future. "The move, *The Kid* really TOUCHED my heart in so many ways" (Rick's uppercase emphasis). Then Rick's excellent mind weighed in as he itemized three elements of the film that made it work. "(1) Russ was the perfect jerk (reminds me of me), (2) Rusty saved the day and the movie, and (3) Amy was so genuine and real—loved her!"

Karen: "I loved the time in the paddle boat with [my friend]. It was a more relaxed time but still sharing and hearing the heart of each of us. Precious time together."

Dave: "Some wonderful friendships have begun. . . . I felt I was heard. . . .*Sacred Sorrow*[16] is such a great book for understanding deep ways of connecting with God. . . .We need to really experience the joy of God's glory. . . . I'm feeling quite connected right now. . . . All of us were very real with each other."

Stan: "The anxiety is relieved and has been replaced by an almost physical sense of the presence of the Master. . . . I can't separate lectio from breath prayer or signature Scripture; I see all as an integrated triad. . . . [Group discussions] are very important for maintaining objectivity. The quiet was welcome time; my mind is too much in control."

Marlee: "I love the image of a spiritual spa, but that does imply some pressure will be applied to some sore spots. . . . One question about the source of contemplation sent me researching to discover that contemplation is 'creating space for observation.' Abram did that—sitting in the door of his tent [when] the visitors arrived."

Ken: It's all about relationship with God. . . . I'm excited about where God is taking me. . . . 'Let your name be Holy.' Wow!"

Robin: "The group discussions were great. They helped me learn as I see others process the material. . . . I really appreciated the tables [in Dennis Fuqua's book, *Living Prayer: The Lord's Prayer Alive in You*[17]] and ways that we can pray each part of the prayer. . . . A stunner for me was looking at how Jesus directed us to call God our Father. I have never really thought about that before. . . . I am finding peace for the first time. God doesn't need to answer prayers the way I ask in order for me to be OK."

Linda: "I felt disconnected from God during the Refresh and Reflect exercise, but I confessed and re-communed with Him little by little. . . . Soul Friendship is real, constructive, effective! . . . I feel compelled to pray for these dear women: relationship stuff again. It helps me feel connected. . . . Learning the biblical and historical perspective reassures me that we're not on some new age branch that in fact, the roots are quite old but have been lost."

Phil: "Refreshing during a drought time. . . .It is joyful to be here with you all. . . I enjoyed focusing on the Father and the various 'thys'. . . . [the Lord's Prayer] is much more about the Father than I realized." About the time reviewing breath prayer and lectio, Phil was enthusiastic: "Sweet! Helpful! Healthy! . . . I loved the biblical and historical background material—I will be reading the ancient and current contemplative writers."

Commenting on the Refresh and Reflect session, Gretchen wrote: "A real issue appeared and I got some answers, and inspiration, and support." In an eighteen point list of insights gained from reading Jan Johnson's, *When the Soul Listens*[18], point four was, "Head and heart knowledge must intersect," and point sixteen was "Contemplative prayer is the opposite of analyzing."

Judith: "Why should I be amazed anymore that God seems to orchestrate the [soul friendship] pairings? Marlee was just what I needed. . . . When we all start abiding together, the juices start to flow. I begin to harmonize/resonate with all the wisdom sitting in this room . . . As always, sitting with kindred spirits so refreshed the deep places."

Charles: "Being an analyzer (perfectionist) isn't always pleasant."

CHAPTER 4

LISTENING TO SCRIPTURE

The Spirit gives life; the flesh counts for nothing. The words I
have spoken to you—they are full of the Spirit and life.
—John 6:63

I started to read the Bible for myself when I was fifteen years old.
A wise pastor at Bible camp challenged us to make a vow to God.
"Look over your life, young people, and make a promise to God.
Decide what you need to do, and commit yourself to make that
change." That week I promised God that I would read his Word
every day. Whether it was like peaches and cream, or shredded
wheat without milk, I would take God's Word into my heart and
mind each day. That promise changed the course of my life. Until
that point, I was prone to an up and down, roller-coaster connection
to God, but over the course of that summer I began to grow steadily.
The Word became a delight and a joy. I remember reading Romans 8
for the first time and writing in the margin of my *Living Bible*, "This
chapter is good!" I started listening to God, and he started forming
more of his life in me. That spring I had toyed with rebellion against
my Christian upbringing. But when school started that September,
I readily responded to an invitation to join a new Christian youth
movement that had come to our campus. I discovered that listening
to God in Scripture is essential for spiritual life and health. God

opened my heart and poured in spiritual truth. I was coming alive in ways that I had never envisioned.

Fast forward ten years. Now I was sitting in seminary classrooms, learning to think deeply about Scripture. The professors were teaching us how to understand the Bible in its original context. They immersed us in ancient cultures, languages, and customs. Once again Scripture became alive to me. In my teen years, God initiated a revolution in my *heart*. Now he was awakening my *mind*. He was teaching me to think accurately about what the biblical authors were saying and how that truth applied to contemporary life. I could understand. I could clarify the biblical message for others. Once again my vision shifted. Once again I responded to a new calling, this time to preach and teach God's people as their pastor.

Now fast forward twenty-five years. Once again I was sitting in a graduate school classroom. This time the professor was teaching the class how to prayerfully meditate on Scripture. Where once I had learned to read the cultural, theological, and grammatical details of a passage, now I was learning to let the Scripture read me. Where once I had learned to organize the message of a passage and turn what I was learning into a sermon to touch the hearts of others, now I found the passages reorganizing my heart. I found a gentle corrective taking place in the inner workings of my soul. I discovered a way to listen to God deeply. In a manner that I had not imagined, I began to discern God's personal presence breathing life within my soul. Once again my vision shifted, and I answered a new call, this time to lead retreats and seminars and to teach at the graduate level.

What is it like when you interact with Scripture? Are you ready for a deepening experience with God through his Word? Good! Let's begin.

God Breathes Out, We Breath In

Praying the Scriptures provides a powerful way for the Holy Spirit to take the living Word that he inspired and penetrate the innermost places of our being—and in those deep places, God calls to us. Speaking of this powerful penetration of our hearts by the Holy Spirit, the writer to the Hebrews states:

> For the word of God is alive and active. Sharper than any double-edged sword, it penetrates even to dividing soul and spirit, joints and marrow; it judges the thoughts and attitudes of the heart. Nothing in all creation is hidden from God's sight. Everything is uncovered and laid bare before the eyes of him to whom we must give account.
>
> —Heb. 4:12–13

When we cannot figure out our motivations or begin to correct our thoughts and attitudes, the living Word opens up the depths of our being before the Wonderful Counselor. In his loving gaze, we find the gentle correction that creates new pathways of thinking, feeling, and acting. The Lord transforms us from the inside out. But how do we allow Scripture to penetrate that far into our inner being?

There are many ways to get Scripture into our minds and hearts. We can all be thankful for the many Bible translations that bring clarity to our reading. We can thank the Lord for preachers and teachers who have, under the leadership of the Holy Spirit, pressed God's Word into our thinking. And we can be thankful for the verses that we've studied, memorized, and pondered throughout our lives. All of these are excellent ways to experience the penetrating voice of God.

The method that opened up a deeper level of communion with God for me personally is the ancient art of lectio divina, or the divine reading of Scripture. Let me explain. Lectio is Latin for reading, and divina simply means divine. In other words, it is a way to read Scripture with an increasing awareness of the presence of God. The goal of lectio divina is to open ourselves to the presence of the Lord through the written text of Scripture. Our mission is to pray our consent to God's intent as he expressed it through his Spirit in the words of the Bible.

Robert M. Mulholland, Jr., dean of the School of Theology and professor of New Testament at Asbury Theological Seminary, heartily encourages the use of lectio divina. He views it as an effective way to participate in God's intent to unfold his truth in the hearts of people. Mulholland sees the inspiration of the writer and the inspiration of the reader as two parts of God's creative work in breathing out the Word. Where others might speak of the Spirit's work of illumination in assisting the reader to apprehend what the biblical writer intended, Mulholland speaks of the reader's participation with the writer in allowing God to breathe his living Word into the soul. He summarizes why lectio is important: "In prayerful, relational/formational reading of Scripture, we become participants in the process of inspiration."[19]

Let me unpack what I believe Mulholland is saying. The Spirit who breathed the very words of God into the hearts and minds of Moses, David, Luke, and Paul now breathes the living words they wrote into the soul of the receptive listener. As the Holy Spirit moved the ancient writers, he now moves within modern readers as they prayerfully ponder the Scriptures. Lectio divina is about breathing in the living Word as the Spirit of God breathes it out. We discover that God's Word lives and acts within us. He informs us of his divine intent, corrects us in our rebellion, and trains us to think, feel, and act for God's good purpose. We find ourselves increasingly equipped for every good work that God intends for us to do. Paul describes the activity of God through his Word:

> All Scripture is God-breathed and is useful for teaching, rebuking, correcting and training in righteousness, so that the servant of God may be thoroughly equipped for every good work.
> —2 Tim. 3:16–17

As with his creation of the first man, Adam, God breathes life into the new creation through his divinely inspired Word.

Peter uses an ancient sailing term to describe the amazing way that the Holy Spirit put his Word into the minds and hearts of the biblical writers:

> Above all, you must understand that no prophecy of Scripture came about by the prophet's own interpretation of things. For

prophecy never had its origin in the human will, but prophets, though human, spoke from God as they were carried along by the Holy Spirit.

—2 Peter 1:20–21

The Greek word translated by the phrase *carried along* refers to the wind in the sails of a ship. Like wind in the sails of an ancient sailing ship, the Holy Spirit moved the writers of Scripture so that what they wrote was exactly what God intended. God moved in the prophets who wrote his living Word, and he moves in those who receive it. The Word lives. Jesus said that these words are life itself:

The Spirit gives life; the flesh counts for nothing. The words I have spoken to you—they are full of the Spirit and life.

—John 6:63

As God breathes life out, we breathe life in. In this way the living Word renews our souls. But we must be yielded. While anyone with a basic education can read the words on the pages of the Bible, hearing God in this way is reserved for those who have yielded their mind, their heart, and their attention to the Master. Jesus said it this way:

Jesus replied, "Anyone who loves me will obey my teaching. My Father will love them, and we will come to them and make our home with them."

—John 14:23

The Father and the Son abide closely with the one who so loves the teachings of Jesus that he desires to obey them from the heart. Lectio is a way to yield to the voice of God and experience the companionship of the Master who speaks.

Thomas Keating writes of lectio as a way of developing friendship with the Lord:

Lectio Divina is the most traditional way of cultivating friendship with Christ. It is a way of listening to the texts of Scripture as if we were in conversation with Christ and he was suggesting the topics of conversation. The daily encounter with Christ and reflection on his word leads beyond mere acquaintanceship to an attitude of friendship, trust, and love. Conversation simplifies and gives way to communing, or as Gregory the Great (sixth century), summarizing the Christian contemplative tradition, put it, "resting in God." This was the classical meaning of contemplative prayer for the first sixteen centuries.[20]

There it is again—communing with God. We are doing more than reading for information here. We are listening to the heartbeat of God.

A Simple Four-Step Method

So how do we do it?

There have been many different styles of lectio down through the ages. In our Awakenings retreats and seminars we use the form of lectio that the Benedictine monks have been using for centuries. The following is our interpretation of the Benedictine form of lectio divina. To enter in, plan to set aside twenty-five to thirty minutes to be still with a particular passage of Scripture. Let's begin with Psalm 131.

A song of ascents. Of David.

My heart is not proud, O LORD,
my eyes are not haughty;
I do not concern myself with great matters
or things too wonderful for me.
But I have stilled and quieted my soul;
like a weaned child with its mother,
like a weaned child is my soul within me.
O Israel, put your hope in the LORD
both now and forevermore.

—Ps. 131: 1–3

Plan to read the passage four times. After each reading, take time to listen to the Lord in a particular way.

The First Reading

During the first reading, take note of a key phrase that stands out to you. Then follow your reading with a few moments of silent meditation upon that phrase. We see this modeled in the biblical writers themselves. The prophet Jeremiah speaks of taking God's words in so deeply that it was like making a meal of them:

> When your words came, I ate them;
> they were my joy and my heart's delight.
>
> —Jer. 15:16

As with any good meal, we savor each bite of truth. The psalmist writes:

> How sweet are your words to my taste,
> sweeter than honey to my mouth!
>
> —Ps. 119:103

So as you read, look for those words that for you are a delight, the words that seem sweet to your taste. Let's say that you have just read Psalm 131, and you notice particularly the line, "I do not concern myself with great matters or things too wonderful for me." As you grow silent with God, you repeat the phrase over and over. You chew on the words as though they were a cut of prime beef. They are, after all, life to your soul. After several moments (I like to give it four or five minutes of silence) you realize that you do have a tendency to concern yourself with great matters. It dawns on you that you tend to mind other people's business and concern yourself with things that are, in fact, beyond you. You realize that God has some correcting to do. But rather than focusing now on how you fall short of God's desire expressed in this verse, keep your attention on the Scripture and press on to the next stage of lectio.

The Second Reading

Now read the psalm again. After your second reading, think through the overview of the passage. What are the major points

43

that the psalmist is touching on? What are the lessons that he is trying to get across? What word pictures and turns of phrase does he use? This is the part where we can use our active minds. While this stage of lectio is not the time for an inductive Bible study on the passage, it does approach that kind of analytical thinking. The old writers called this stage *meditatio*.

Psalm 1 describes the life of one who meditates upon the word of God:

> Blessed is the one
> who does not walk in step with the wicked
> or stand in the way that sinners take
> or sit in the company of mockers,
> but whose delight is in the law of the LORD,
> and who meditates on his law day and night.
> That person is like a tree planted by streams of water,
> which yields its fruit in season
> and whose leaf does not wither—
> whatever they do prospers.
>
> —Ps. 1:1–3

As the Lord commanded Joshua, we are called to think constantly upon his Word:

> Keep this Book of the Law always on your lips; meditate on it day and night so that you will be careful to do everything written in it. Then you will be prosperous and successful.
>
> —Josh. 1:8

So you have read Psalm 131 for the second time, and you think things through. You scan the passage again and notice how this is a Psalm of David, and that it was a song of ascents. You wonder what that title might mean and decide to look it up later. You see that David is talking about a heart that is not proud and does not overreach its proper boundaries. You especially appreciate this after your insights from the first reading and meditation time. You see that David has somehow quieted his soul, and that he compares that to a weaned child with its mother. And at the end you see an exhortation for the whole nation of Israel to put their hope in the Lord. You sit still with these thoughts for four or five minutes, not writing them down, but just thinking.

As you think about David's commitment to getting his soul to quiet down, you notice the sound of the air conditioner going on and off. You think, "I should set the thermostat a little higher," and you start to get up and do it. But you realize that you are not too cold, and decide to just stay still. So you release the thought about the air conditioner, and return to your ruminations on the Psalm. "Let's see, stilled and quieted my soul. . . . A weaned child with its mother." An image of quiet rest emerges within you, and you begin to feel a sense of being more settled than at first. Then you notice that the five minutes are about up (I like to use the timer on my cell phone), and you are ready to move on to the next movement of lectio.

The Third Reading

At this stage you read the psalm again and then take time to silently pray back to the Lord what you've been noticing from the passage. Talk with the Lord especially about what you see that he intends for you from this passage. Speak out whatever you need to say to the Lord about this particular Word of his. As you pray, you recall how he underlined the part about not being concerned for the things he has assigned to others, the things that are beyond you. And so you say, "Lord, you know how I often wonder what the elders were thinking with that decision about the youth pastor. I know I didn't have an inside track on what happened there, and that they had a responsibility to do what was best for the youth and their parents. I just wasn't in on the information they had. I'm wondering now if I judged their decision unfairly. Please train me, Lord, to keep my attention on the things you have entrusted to me, and I will trust you to lead others who have responsibilities that are beyond mine. And that part about presenting you with a stilled and quieted soul—I admit that my soul is all over the place. I seem to be anxious about so many things all at once! I really struggle to slow down and pay attention. Please keep working with me here.

I see from this verse that it is my responsibility to quiet my soul. I'm going to need your help with that. And that part about hope? I need help from outside of myself if I am going to make progress with this. I put my hope in you, Lord. Only you can do this in me. Thank you. Through Jesus I pray this, amen."

Now you notice that you have a couple of more minutes in this third stage of lectio. So you pray about the picture of the quieted child and ask the Lord to help you lay back and just rest with him. As you do, you feel that sense of stillness expanding in your soul, a peace that you have not noticed in a long, long time. When the timer rings, you realize that you have been in a very refreshing place with Jesus.

Now you are ready to enter the fourth stage of lectio divina.

The Fourth Reading

During this reading, seek out a single word from the text that summarizes God's intent for you at this time. Then sit quietly, using that key word to focus your attention upon the presence of the Lord. Imagine him breathing this one word toward you—a word that provides a gift of immeasurable value. Breathe in that one word, and take it into your soul. As you breathe in this word, breathe out your one word—your word of consent, your personal yes to Jesus. Pray the prayer that Mary prayed when the angel announced that she would bear the Son of God: "May it be unto me as you have said."[21]

Another aspect of this fourth stage is to simply enjoy being present with the Lord.

At this point in the lectio, everything has been said and done. God has breathed out his Word to you, and you have spoken back to God in prayer. Now nothing more needs to be said. There is only the need to be quiet with God and enjoy the deep satisfaction of this amazing relationship. The God who loves you with an everlasting love has moved heaven and earth so that he can sit with you in holiness.

Let me tell you a story that for me expresses what this fourth stage of lectio is like. Jessica Nielson Reurich is like a daughter to my wife Kathryn and me. She lived with us for a couple of years before she went off to Capernwray Bible College and met her husband, Jeremy. Now they serve with Urban Promise, a mission reaching inner city children and their families in Toronto, Canada. On the occasion of our twenty-fifth wedding anniversary, Jessica achieved complete surprise when she travelled clear across North America to attend our celebration. We will never forget that moment when she appeared at the door of the reception hall carrying twenty-five silver balloons. "Jessica, what are you doing here?" I asked.

"Fulfilling the duties of a daughter," she said. She completely blew us away.

As I think about the gift that she and Jeremy gave to Kathryn and me that day, three moments are especially precious. The first was the moment Jessica walked in the door! The second was when Kathryn, Jessica, and I held hands and walked through the crowd. And the third was when we simply sat together at the end of the program, looking out at the people in the room. We were not talking, we were just being together. And what do you suppose Kathryn and I were feeling at that moment? We felt extremely loved, honored, and respected by Jessica and Jeremy. They had made a sacrificial gift. All that was left for us to do was to enjoy it.

It is this sitting quietly together that for me expresses what this final movement of lectio is about. The first three movements have prepared us for this moment. Just as all of Jessica and Jeremy's planning provided the way for her to come and be with us, so God has taken countless sacrificial steps so that he can quietly abide with those he has redeemed. God has sent Jesus to sacrifice himself for our sins and open the pathway of intimate communion. He sent the Spirit who inspired his holy Word and has opened our hearts and minds to receive Jesus as Savior and receive the Word implanted. And now we have pondered his Word and spoken back to God in prayer. For the moment, nothing more needs to be said. We simply need to be quiet with him and enjoy the deep satisfaction of this amazing relationship with the God who loves us with a universe-rending love.

Take time now to select one word from Psalm 131 that for you expresses God's intention at this moment in your life. As you breathe it in, breathe out your heart's consent. And as you abide with him, let all the words grow still. Seek to be aware of the presence of him who has moved heaven and earth so that he could commune with you. Take up to ten minutes for this final movement in the lectio cycle. Be still and aware of the living God.

Journaling

After your final season of silence, take time to write about what this experience has been like for you. First, reflect on what it was like to be silent. Write about where you may have struggled with the method. Think about any insights that come to mind about how to be silent and receptive to the Lord. Then write down your key phrase and what it meant to you. Write also about what you noticed in the overview of the psalm. Pray even as you write, asking God to remind you of the thoughts and feelings that you experienced during your time with him. Take time to write about your key word, and what it was like to ponder that word. Finish by recording any sense you gained of the Lord's presence. Even if it was just a fleeting moment, record what that moment was like.

Next Steps

Take time over the coming days to practice additional sessions of lectio on Psalm 131. That's right; as you pray repeatedly over the same passage of Scripture, the Holy Spirit is able to breathe more deeply into your soul. You will discover a greater experience of refreshing, challenging, and corrective truth moving into your soul. Thomas Keating reminds us to respect the fruit of lectio that grows steadily over a season. He writes, "The ripe fruit of the regular practice of lectio divina is assimilating the word of God and being assimilated by it. It is a movement from conversation to communion."[22] Giving our attention to several lectio sessions on the same Scripture provides God the opportunity to grow his fruit within the orchard of our soul and thus achieve his purpose in us.

Also, seek ways to integrate lectio into your regular Bible reading and study times. During your reading, you might take a few minutes to meditate on one section of the chapter. If you are preparing to teach a section of Scripture, you will find that practicing a session of lectio on that passage adds special depth to your understanding.

In a few minutes you will be asked to reflect on your experience of praying Psalm 131. Do you have your journal handy? Before you write your thoughts, consider the following Refection on Reflection blog written by Theresa Schaudies and posted on the Awakenings Prayer website.

I was reading a dead, boring tome on theories of organizational change for a class I'm taking when I was surprised by an obscure reference to the power of reflection. My heavy-lidded eyes popped open, and I sat up as I reread the paragraph. Here is what it said: [F]our rules that . . . change leaders [leaders of change] should accept to enhance their self-development:

1. You are your own best teacher.
2. You accept responsibility and blame no one.
3. You can learn anything you want to learn.
4. True understanding comes from reflection on your experience.[23]

Theologically, there might be a problem with rule number one, since a biblical view of the heart of self is that it is deceptive and desperately wicked (Jer. 17:9). I would revise rule number one to read, "short of divine sources of instruction, your own council is at least as reliable as another's." I'm not giving up on the possibility of divine instruction: The Sovereign Lord has given me an instructed tongue to know the word that sustains the weary. Morning by morning he wakens me—wakens my ear to listen like one being taught.

—Isa. 50:4

But let's look at rule number four. True understanding comes from reflection on your experience. What happens when you pray Scripture through the four cycles of lectio divina? How many levels and kinds of understanding are rising up, penetrating your brain and your heart and your soul when you yield to deep, silent reflection? Then the act of translating the spiritual experience into the English language as you write in your journal is yet another round that leads to deeper understanding. Maybe we should call the journaling we do after praying Scripture stage five lectio.

Ask yourself, would your experience of lectio divina garner the same intense sense of meaning and connection with God if you skipped the journaling? Sometimes I'm tempted to do that. My time in silence was sweet and my mind and body are still. Journaling takes movement, activity . . . but I am always, always rewarded when I make the transition from stillness to writing because my mind lights up with the effort. No, I can't capture all the richness of my time in lectio, but I can record a brief snippet of it. This brief snippet is there to be enjoyed and built upon. It is a picture of understanding.

Walter Bennis says that reflection is an important part of self-development. I think it is also an important part of spiritual development. Especially when the instruction comes from the Lord. Now that is an experience worth reflecting on. Are you up for that?[24]

Reflection

Reflect now on what you gained from your lectio time in Psalm 131. How is this experience different from the ways you have approached Scripture in the past?

How is what you gained through your lectio time different from other methods of Bible study?

How would you describe your experience of lectio to a person who has not yet prayed over Scripture in this way?

API Participants Respond

About doing lectio on Isaiah 50:4, "The Sovereign Lord has given me an instructed tongue to know the word that sustains the weary," Charles commented. "I've done it before—more than once. Always love to do it again! There is no end to the value of those words." And at another time he wrote, "Lectio has already proven powerful in the past—nearly frightening on occasion."

At the end of the very first seminar in October, Robin wrote specifically about praying Psalm 131: "Loved this! Felt like the Holy Spirit really met me and showed (revealed) new things to me." In November she said: "I like revisiting the Scripture over and over as I get new insights." At the second retreat in February, she said, "Lectio is so meaningful. I get insights that I never would have seen without it." Author's note: for many years, Robin has maintained a discipline of memorizing Scripture.

At the second retreat, Stan wrote of lectio divina: "Silent meditation upon a larger picture inspired by signature verses [was the most meaningful of the devotional practices experienced there.]" But he has some struggles as well, "The lack of time to write between readings of the passage was hard for me. I'm not confident of holding onto the 'flashes of insight' once the next reading begins."

Of doing lectio on Psalm 131, Ken said: "Doing this forced me to truly listen to what the Holy Spirit was saying to me." Later Ken singled out lectio as the devotional practice he found most meaningful. "I actually enjoyed lectio the most. [I'm] learning to listen to God the Holy Spirit while reading Scripture—then re-reading." According to the end-of-year survey, he continues to practice lectio as a part of his regular devotional pattern.

After doing lectio on John 10:1–5 (Jesus the Good Shepherd), Marlee shared this: "I like that we can identify Jesus because he follows protocol. No question about who is attempting to lead us and to speak to us." On another occasion she wrote: "I gained so much insight in journaling and reflecting later. I began to see the 'path' emerging—and the paver of the path." Later we took a prayer walk with our lectio passage. Marlee continued to gain insight. "I walked our path, being directed where to walk, realizing with me it was always about the walking path. I love to walk with my camera slung around my neck looking to discern the path—knowing that what seems to start in the physical is really started in the spiritual because there is a path of peace I am to walk and carry for the presence of God."

Rick wrote, "All sessions of lectio are always excellent!" Rick has developed his own style of praying Scripture. He reads just one book of the Bible every week for a whole year and then engages with the book through contemplative prayer and intercession.

Dave has also incorporated lectio into his devotional life. Of the introduction to lectio with Psalm 131 he wrote: "It was a great procedure for really focusing on the Scripture in a meaningful way. Redirecting my thoughts when my mind wandered—I really was able to experience what the Holy Spirit had for me."

Linda indicated on a feedback sheet that she rarely did lectio at home, "But I like it a lot! Just need some discipline to do it. Eventually I want to teach this to someone. . . . As usual, I felt I couldn't get any more [out of the lectio passage], but then I did!"

Of lectio on Psalm 131, Karen said: "This time helped me to slow down and focus on Scripture. This is something I have a hard time doing—slowing down and focusing." She wrote that the most meaningful part of the first retreat was, "doing lectio on the passage that I chose." In January we did lectio on the Lord's Prayer. Karen wrote: "It is fresh every time I do it. It is amazing how you read the same passage at different times and God speaks fresh and new each time." She has taught lectio to others and continues to use it in her devotional times.

Phil wrote that he felt a "healthy closeness and peace in the Lord when so much was turbulent and troubling." After doing lectio on the devotional, *Morning, Noon and Night,*[25] Phil wrote: "I enjoyed 'experiencing' the persons of the Trinity in a quiet prayer time."

Judith practices her own version of lectio at home on a regular basis but enjoys the discipline of doing it in the API group setting. "I tend to be very scattered. It is a tremendous help for me when someone limits/categorizes/directs my squandered energy."

Of lectio on Isaiah 50:4–5 Gretchen said: "The prayer model is powerful. The Scripture is powerful. I was nourished." With Psalm 139 she wrote: "I really felt enlightened by the passage, and what I heard will stay with me. . . . The lectio helped to center me *and* de-center me! The de-centering at least was honest and from myself. I will just keep praying."

Some Final Thoughts

Let me (Wes) share a few of the insights I have gained through numerous sessions of lectio on Psalm 131. (You may want to reflect on the psalm yourself a few more times before you read my reflections.)

First, David, the psalmist, was a great king; he had many things to be concerned about, yet he recognized that some things were beyond him. He had mastered the posture of a weaned child, a child who was content in the presence of his mother; a child who was not grasping and demanding his next meal from his mother's breast. Rather, he had smoothed out the longings in his soul, he had stilled and quieted his inner self such that he was able to be at rest in the presence of the one who sustains and nurtures him. He had developed a quieted and composed spirit. Rather than squirming and sighing, his soul was satisfied and still.

The weaned child is an apt metaphor for this state of tranquility. A child at the breast knows only one way of nurture. When that child is hungry, only one method of feeding will do. But the child who has been weaned learns that his mother now has a multitude of ways to feed him. This child has been trained to stop crying for his mother's milk. He has learned to stop clinging and demanding what his mother used to freely supply. Now he has learned a quiet contentment.

Believers who enter into deep stillness with God understand that God has ways to nurture them that they have not experienced in the past. For this reason, the psalm urges seekers to be still, to ease up, to not concern themselves with issues that are beyond them but to cease striving and rest in God.

Let me share a final reflection from St. John of the Cross, a great mystic of the church. St. John used the image of the weaned child to illustrate the progress in detachment from a self-indulgent spirituality: "The tiny infant must be cosseted, suckled, and carried everywhere, but as it begins to grow it must be weaned from the cozy breast to take solid food, and put down to walk on its own feet."[26] Thus, the disciple learns detachment from, "spiritual vices: self-regarding desire for the externals of worship and for those consolations of religion which feed the human ego."[27] God thus communicates himself directly to the Christian, "without the medium of intelligible or imaginable thought."[28]

Imagine your soul no longer as a dependent infant clinging to its mother, but as a robust little boy or rambunctious little girl, heading out into a myriad of adventures. Let lectio be for you an invitation to grow in maturity with the Lord.

CHAPTER 5

CREATING OUR BREATH PRAYER

PRAYING GOD'S CHARACTER, MISSION, AND OUR SOUL'S DEEP NEED

Pray continually.
—1 Thess. 5:17

Steve and Diane Mosman were veteran missionary educators waiting upon God for a new ministry assignment. This transition eventually led them into a greatly expanded ministry role. During the time of waiting, Diane began to pray, "Abba Father, carry me." This prayer arose as Diane pondered one of the lowest seasons of her life on the mission field: a time of waiting that involved a serious health condition and the necessity of returning to the United States. As she reflected back to this time of weakness and deep dependency on God, she summarized her soul's deep need in this profoundly simple prayer of the heart. She needed to know that Abba Father was holding her close and moving her forward when she felt most vulnerable and in need of strength.

During these days she was praying lectio divina over Habakkuk 2:1–3:

> I will stand at my watch
> and station myself on the ramparts;
> I will look to see what he will say to me,
> and what answer I am to give to this complaint.

Then the LORD replied:

"Write down the revelation
and make it plain on tablets
so that a herald may run with it.
For the revelation awaits an appointed time;
it speaks of the end and will not prove false.
Though it linger, wait for it;
it will certainly come and will not delay."

These ancient words from God to his anxious prophet Habakkuk brought encouragement to Diane as she waited on the Lord. As Diane prayed, she reflected in her journal: "The Lord wants us to station ourselves where we can look and see and listen to what God will speak to us (when he does answer) for 2006 and beyond." God would give the vision at the proper time, "all we needed to do was wait patiently again for the appointed time, believing it won't be false. . . . We must live by faith."

The outcome of Diane's prayers over this text was a deep peace that characterized the entire transition. "This time we have not been uptight at all, even though waiting was hard." Diane was doing lectio on this text on June 26, 2006, and the new ministry assignment came on June 27, with the confirmation of the call coming on July 11. Diane's notes from her journal on June 26 reflect the challenge of the Habakkuk passage: "Keep calling even if it seems he isn't answering you. Stand watch and look and see what God will say to you. Write down the revelation . . . so that others who read may run with it . . . live by faith!"

Her key word for her lectio that day was *write*. On July 15 Diane wrote, "looking at the June 26 journal entry now, I can hardly believe it was written the day before we met Jamie Farr of Wycliffe Bible Translators and he suggested the Children's Education Coordinators' job to us just out of the blue, unexpected even to him, it seems." It is clear that God was processing Steve and Diane's next ministry assignment in real time as Diane was praying over this text. He led them into seven fruitful years overseeing the educational needs of the children of Wycliffe families in Africa.

Diane had combined lectio divina with a form of prayer that the ancients called *breath prayer*. Let me ask you—what do you need most from God at this season of your life? How would you express that in a short prayer?

The Origin of Breath Prayer

I was introduced to breath prayer during my first spiritual direction appointment. My mentor taught me to combine the deep need of my heart with a name of the Lord that reveals his supreme ability to meet just that type of need. This kind of prayer was first developed and practiced by the Christian monks and hermits of the third and fourth centuries. These desert saints were pursuing constant contact with the Lord in obedience to Paul's command to pray without ceasing (1 Thess. 5:17). They also drew from Luke 18:13 where Jesus tells the story of the penitent tax collector who, "would not even look up to heaven, but beat his breast and said, 'God, have mercy on me, a sinner.'" Jesus assured his listeners that this man went home justified. The ancients envisioned his constant plea rising to the Father, and they joined him in his prayer. From this text they developed what came to be known as the Jesus Prayer and made it their habit to pray it repeatedly—"Lord Jesus Christ, have mercy on me, a sinner."

Several other New Testament passages provide models of this kind of repetitive, focused entreaty to the Lord. Consider the repeated cry of Bartimaeus as he appealed to the Lord Jesus to have mercy upon him. Mark 10:46–48 records the story this way:

> Then they came to Jericho. As Jesus and his disciples, together with a large crowd, were leaving the city, a blind man, Bartimaeus (that is, the Son of Timaeus), was sitting by the roadside begging. When he heard that it was Jesus of Nazareth, he began to shout, "Jesus, Son of David, have mercy on me! Many rebuked him and told him to be quiet, but he shouted all the more, "Son of David, have mercy on me!"

Bartimaeus called out, addressing the Lord with a name that revealed his faith in Jesus as Messiah King. Bartimaeus believed that only Jesus, the Son of David, the Messiah could meet his need. He persisted in calling upon the Lord, even though the crowd sought to silence him.

Another gospel example is the Canaanite woman who entered into a theological debate with the Savior to persuade him to free her daughter from a demon. This desperate mother would not be deterred from making her plea to the Lord:

> Leaving that place, Jesus withdrew to the region of Tyre and Sidon. A Canaanite woman from that vicinity came to him, crying out, "Lord, Son of David, have mercy on me! My daughter is suffering terribly from demon possession." Jesus did not answer a word. So his disciples came to him and urged him, "Send her away, for she keeps crying out after us." He answered, "I was sent only to the lost sheep of Israel." The woman came and knelt before him. "Lord, help me!" she said. He replied, "It is not right to take the children's bread and toss it to their dogs." "Yes, Lord," she said, "but even the dogs eat the crumbs that fall from their masters' table." Then Jesus answered, "Woman, you have great faith! Your request is granted." And her daughter was healed from that very hour.
>
> —Matt. 15:21–28

As she builds her case for her daughter, evidence of this woman's faith is clear in that she calls Jesus the Son of David. Like Bartimaeus, she believed in his identity as the Messiah King—the Promised One—God's anointed leader for the nations. She was compelled by a need so strong that she would not be put off. Jesus' words make him seem hard to get, and yet in the end, impressed by her persistent faith, he meets her need. Warren Wiersbe clarifies the Lord's intention: "Jesus was not playing games with this woman, nor was he trying to make the situation more difficult. He was drawing out of her a growing response of faith."[29] Persisting in the prayer of the heart is an expression of our resolute faith in Jesus.

Consider also the Lord's own experience in the Garden of Gethsemane. Recall his anguished hours before going to the cross. Remember his three-fold appeal to his Father.

"My Father, if it is possible, may this cup be taken from me. Yet not as I will, but as you will." Then he returned to his disciples and found them sleeping. "Could you men not keep watch with me for one hour?" he asked Peter. "Watch and pray so that you will not fall into temptation. The spirit is willing, but the body is weak."

He went away a second time and prayed, "My Father, if it is not possible for this cup to be taken away unless I drink it, may your will be done."

When he came back, he again found them sleeping, because their eyes were heavy. So he left them and went away once more and prayed the third time, saying the same thing.

—Matt. 26:39–44

What can we learn from this intimate view into the prayer life of Jesus? I want to suggest at least four elements that we find here in and in other biblical texts that can help us give form to the deeply held prayers of our own hearts.

The Four Elements of Breath Prayer

The first is the name of the Lord. Calling upon the name of the Lord puts his people in a place of great strength. As Proverbs puts it:

The name of the Lord is a fortified tower;
the righteous run to it and are safe.

—Prov. 18:10

The psalmist writes:

Some trust in chariots and some in horses,
but we trust in the name of the LORD our God.

—Ps. 20:7

Isaiah calls upon the people of God to tell of his mighty works and celebrate the power of his name:

In that day you will say:
"Give thanks to the LORD, call on his name;

make known among the nations what he has done,
and proclaim that his name is exalted."

—Isa. 12:4

What does it mean when God's people call upon his name?

In his classic *Theology of the Old Testament*, Gustav Oehler writes of how the God of the Old Testament reveals his names in order to engage the needs of the people with whom He is in covenant: "In short, God names Himself, not according to what He is for Himself, but *to what He is for man* . . ."[30] In other words, the divine purpose in God's self-revelation of his names is so that people with whom he makes covenant will know who he is in light of their need. By revealing himself in these concrete ways, God invites believers to call upon him as the God who is present in history in particular ways to meet particular needs.

When we call upon the name of the Lord, we are appealing to the character of the one who has chosen to reveal himself to us in sacred Scripture. We are taking the Lord up on his amazing offer to be in covenant with us. Let's think about the New Testament examples we've mentioned.

In Gethsemane, Jesus appealed to God as Father, specifically, *my father*. Today we are accustomed to addressing God as Father, but the devout Jews of Jesus' day were scandalized by his habit of addressing God in such a familiar way. But in his anguished prayer, Jesus called upon God as Father because by doing so he emphasized his intimate relation with God. Richard Foster in his wonderful book, *Prayer, Finding the Heart's True Home*, speaks of the amazing privilege of addressing God as Father:

> No, it is not the parental image of God that startles us as we read the Gospels; it is the invitation to address God in such a personal and intimate way that is entirely new. The disciples must have been stunned by the response to their request to be instructed about prayer, for Jesus says simply, "When you pray say: 'Father . . .'" (Luke 11:2). To the faithful Jew who even hesitated to speak the Divine Name, the childlike intimacy of Jesus' words must have been utterly shocking."[31]

Jesus cries out to God as his Father. Both the Canaanite woman and blind Bartimaeus gave evidence of their great faith in the Lord Jesus when they addressed him as the Son of David. They trusted the character of one they believed to be their Messiah King. When we call upon the name of the Lord, we proclaim our trust in his divinely revealed character. So the first element of breath prayer is the name of the Lord.

The second element is the soul's deep need. Jesus called upon God as Father because only the Father could comfort his Son while at the same time affirming to him that the cross was the only way to accomplish the mission of salvation. Bartimaeus called upon Jesus as Son of David because he knew only the Messiah King could grant him the mercy he so desperately sought. The Canaanite woman was desperate for the Son of David to heal her daughter. When we get in touch with our soul's deep need, we take a step into the heart of God. For every need of our soul, there is a marvelous aspect of God's character that tells us He is very good at meeting that need. Let me share some further examples.

Jeremy Reurich directs the internship program for Urban Promise, an inner city ministry to immigrant families in Toronto. When I asked him what he needed most from the Lord, he answered, "I need to see what he's doing so I can join him." He needed to have a sense of what God was doing in the lives of his interns as he trained and directed them. His breath prayer became, "Good Shepherd, alert me to your actions." As Jeremy reflected on John 10, where Jesus speaks of his role as the Good Shepherd, his awareness of what the Lord was doing in the lives of his interns increased.

A seminary student was feeling condemnation for past sins. His prayer became, "Lord My Righteousness, make me feel as clean as you say I am." With repeated prayer over Psalm 51, the penitent's psalm, he was able to see that the guilt in his soul was completely covered by the blood of Christ and he came to a place of deep cleansing.

My brother Gary Johnson was leading his family through a dark valley of suffering. His son Jeremy was in the fight of his life against brain cancer. Gary's longing was for the presence of the Lord to be with them each step of the journey. So his prayer became, "Good Shepherd, walk with us through this suffering." As Gary meditated on Psalm 23, the Lord granted clarity, courage, and wisdom for the long journey.

Many other examples could be shared. What about your need? What do you need most from God at this season of your life?

- Take a moment just now and ask yourself, "What do I need most from God at this time in my life?" Write your response in your journal.
- Now carefully review what you have written. Edit your need down to a single item. If you identified several needs, set all but one aside for later prayer. For now, isolate your one most compelling need. Perhaps it is for guidance, for a sense God's presence, for reassurance, or comfort. Isolate one core need and express it as simply as you can.
- Now prayerfully review the names of God listed at the end of this chapter. As you pray, ask the Holy Spirit to guide you to the name of the Lord that shows you he is attuned to the need of your soul. What name of God meets the deep need of your life today? Write it down in your journal.

It could be that more than one name of the Lord seems to resonate with your soul's deep need. If so, you will want to try out each name with your breath prayer. Take a fifteen-minute walk or go work a bit in your shop, garden, or kitchen. As you do, pray your breath prayer. See how it feels. Let the prayer settle in. Work toward simplicity. Remember, if you are pressed by more than one need, you can create other breath prayers at a later time.

Now that you've identified your soul's deep need and the name of the Lord that shows you how he excels at meeting such a need, let's look at the other two aspects of the breath prayer.

The third aspect of the prayer is compliance to the mission of God. Submit your breath prayer to the mission of God as revealed in Scripture. Notice how Jesus tempers his request with a declaration of allegiance to the saving mission of the Father: "Yet not as I will, but as you will." Bartimaeus' plea for mercy is clearly in line with the mission of Christ to "proclaim freedom for the prisoners and recovery of sight to the blind" (Luke 4:18). The Canaanite woman debates with Jesus, making her case that healing her daughter is consistent with Christ's mission. In each of the modern examples shared above, each seeker immersed their breath prayer into a passage of Scripture that demonstrated God's greater purpose. As you pray your breath prayer, make sure what you are asking is on target with God's mission. If you are not sure, seek counsel with a wise mentor.

The fourth characteristic of breath prayer is repetition. Like the desert fathers and mothers, use your prayer as a way to "pray without ceasing." Notice that Jesus repeats his Gethsemane prayer three times. Bartimaeus persists in his request of Jesus, so much so that "Many rebuked him and told him to be quiet, but he shouted all the more, 'Son of David, have mercy on me!'" Even though Jesus seemed to put her off, the Canaanite woman persisted in her urgent request.

An additional example from Scripture may be helpful. In Jesus' parable of the penitent tax collector, we see the four essential elements of breath prayer:

> To some who were confident of their own righteousness and looked down on everybody else, Jesus told this parable: "Two men went up to the temple to pray, one a Pharisee and the other a tax collector. The Pharisee stood up and prayed about himself: 'God, I thank you that I am not like other men—robbers, evildoers, adulterers—or even like this tax collector. I fast twice a week and give a tenth of all I get.' But the tax collector stood at a distance. He would not even look up to heaven, but beat his breast and said, 'God, have mercy on me, a sinner.' I tell you that this man, rather than the other, went home justified before God. For everyone who exalts himself will be humbled, and he who humbles himself will be exalted."
>
> —Luke 18:9–14

Like the prayer of Bartimaeus and the Canaanite woman, we see that the tax collector appealed to the name of the Lord, he expressed his soul's deep need, and he kept at it. This man knew that he was in great need of mercy, and so he beat his breast repeatedly and pled with God. It was a simple, focused prayer of the heart.

For centuries, the Eastern Orthodox Church has used these and other Scriptures to form what is known as the Jesus Prayer: "Lord Jesus Christ, Son of God, have mercy on me, a sinner." Steven Peter Tsichlis points out how the Jesus Prayer is rooted in the name of the Lord and taps in to the power, glory, and purposes of God:

> The Jesus Prayer is rooted in the Name of the Lord. In the Scriptures, the power and glory of God are present in his Name. In the Old Testament to deliberately and attentively invoke God's Name was to place oneself in his Presence. Jesus, whose name in Hebrew means God saves, is the living Word addressed to humanity. Jesus is the final Name of God. Jesus is *the Name which is above all other names* and it is written that *"all beings should bend the knee at the Name of Jesus"* (Phil. 2:9–10). In this Name devils are cast out (Luke 10:17), prayers are answered (John 14:13-14) and the lame are healed (Acts 3:6–7). The Name of Jesus is unbridled spiritual power."[32]

Tsichlis traces the prayer to its roots in the gospels:

> The words of the Jesus Prayer are themselves based on Scriptural texts: the cry of the blind man sitting at the side of the road near Jericho, "Jesus, Son of David, have mercy on me" (Luke 18:38); the ten lepers who "called to him, 'Jesus, Master, take pity on us'" (Luke 17:13); and the cry for mercy of the publican, "God, be merciful to me, a sinner."
>
> —Luke 18:14[33]

Thus the Jesus Prayer becomes a model for all breath prayer. It is short, it appeals to the name of the Lord, it addresses the deepest need of the soul (forgiveness and cleansing), and it is made for repetition. After I had been praying my first breath prayer for a month, I went to see my spiritual director. "How long do I keep this prayer going?" I asked. "For as long as you need it," she said. Keep your prayer until you sense that God has met the need in your soul. It may be several days, weeks, or even years. Return to your prayer as often as you need it.

In conclusion, breath prayer can be compared to:

- A voicemail—you leave a short message with God until you can have the extended conversation with him that you need.
- The topic sentence of a paragraph—it introduces the conversation you need to have with the Lord.
- A link on a web page—it opens up a whole new vista of relevant information.
- A mobile roadside mechanic—it fixes you up at the side of the road until you can get to the shop for more extended repairs.

Draw from the brief list below to identify the name of God that resonates with your soul's deep need. Also consider the names of Jesus or the Holy Spirit as they are revealed in the Old and New Testaments. The list below will get you started.

Names of God in Scripture

Elohim: The plural form of *EL*, meaning "strong one." It is a plural of majesty and intimates the trinity. It is especially used of God's sovereignty, creative work, mighty works (Gen. 1:1–31; Isa. 45:18; Deut. 5:23–27; 8:10–18; Isa. 54:1–8; Jer. 32:26–31).

Compounds of *El*:

- *El Shaddai*: "God Almighty." Stresses God's abundant, loving supply; He is the all-powerful God who brings generations of blessing out of emptiness and lack of faith. He corrects, chastens, blesses and protects his own (Gen. 17:1–27; 28:1–5; 35:9–15; Ps. 91:1–16).
- *El Elyon*: "The Most High God." Stresses God's strength, sovereignty, and supremacy over earthly kings and kingdoms (Gen. 14:1–20; Ps. 9:1–10; Dan. 4:28–37; Luke 1:32–35).

- *El Roi:* "The Living One Who Sees Me." God sees us when we are far from home; he meets us where we are and gives us a future and a hope (Gen. 16:1–16).

Yahweh (YHWH): The sacred, personal name of Israel's God. The name comes from the verb which means "to exist, be." Thus Yahweh is the source of all being, the self-existent Savior God who is ever present with his people, working out his covenant of redemption (Gen. 4:1–9; Ex. 3:1–15; Ps. 103:1–13).

Compounds of *Yahweh:* These compound titles reveal additional facts about God's character.

- *Yahweh Jireh (Yireh):* "The Lord Sees, the Lord Will Provide." Stresses God's provision for His people (Gen. 22:1–19).
- *Yahweh Nissi:* "The Lord Is My Banner." Stresses that God is our rallying point and our means of victory; the one who fights for His people (Ex. 17:8–16).
- *Yahweh Shalom:* "The Lord Is Peace." Points to the Lord as the only means of our peace when we face overwhelming odds (Judg. 6:1–24).
- *Yahweh Sabbaoth:* "The Lord of Hosts." He is the commander of the armies of heaven (1 Sam. 1:1–20; 17:41–50; 2 Kings 6:15–16; Ps. 46:6–7; Isa. 9:6–7).
- *Yahweh Ro'hi:* "The Lord My Shepherd." The Lord cares for his people as a shepherd guides and protects his sheep (Ps. 23:1–6; John 10:1–30).
- *Yahweh Tsidkenu:* "The Lord our Righteousness." The Lord is the means of our righteousness (Jer. 23:1–6; Rom. 3:21–24).
- *Yahweh Shammah:* "The Lord Is There." Portrays the Lord's personal presence (Ezek. 37:20–28 and Ezek. 48:35).
- *Yahweh Elohim Israel:* "The Lord, the God of Israel." Identifies Yahweh as the God of Israel in contrast to the false gods of the nations (Judg. 5:1–5; Isa 17:4–14).

Abba, Father: The distinctive New Testament revelation— through faith in Christ, God becomes our personal Father. Father is used of God in the Old Testament only fifteen times (for example Psalm 68:4–6, "Father of the Fatherless") while it is used of God 245 times in the New Testament. Abba stresses God's loving care, provision, discipline, and authority (Matt. 7:9–11; James 1:17; Heb. 12:4–12; John 15:15–17; 16:23–24; Eph. 2:13–18 and 3:14–19).[34]

API Participants Respond

In her first year Karen wrote that "It was hard to be honest with myself [about my need]. I have taken care of everyone else's needs but to put down what I need was really hard." However, at the beginning of the second year Karen wrote, "I loved this time. I needed to identify what I needed from God . . . I can use [this breath prayer] any time or place. . . . Being able to verbalize my breath prayer was difficult and emotional but good." She describes how one breath prayer changed over time, "from needing to be carried by my Good Shepherd to needing him to lead me." She also has continued to use breath prayers and different names for God in her prayers very often and has taught breath prayer to others.

Dave: "Good to start with breath prayer—it helps me to really think about my deepest need from God at this time. About the breath prayer presentation by Dr. Phil Templeton, Dave said, "Good! I appreciate how he applied breath prayer to his personal life." Dave has also continued to use breath prayers on a regular basis.

Marlee has been going through a time of simplifying things in her life and saw value in keeping the breath prayer very short. "It helps me to focus."

Robin wrote about her current breath prayer: "The Lord is my Shepherd, I have all that I need." "[I'm] learning to rest in and trust in his provision for me. The name of the Lord as Creator also really struck me. I love God's creation and just love to enjoy it. I love the neighbor's many varieties of bees that visit my garden. I marvel at how beautiful they are. I also think that when I create something—music, art, a project of some kind, how I love it. I keep wanting to look at it and enjoy it. And I got a glimpse of how God must love us, his creation! Those bees reflect the beauty of God as they go about their business. I want to be comfortable in who God created me to be, and know that he loves me."

Coming up with a breath prayer is often a problem for Charles. He says, "There are too many choices. [But] always good results, one way or another. I often use several of the names of God that fit the nature of my prayer—and others that I make up as I go along that describe the God I worship as I have experienced him."

Ken reports that he continues to use breath prayers he developed over the API year and that he often matches one of God's many titles with the nature of his prayer.

Once we had an assignment to write a breath prayer for our whole life. Phil said, "I 'saw' what was needed in the previous years and what I needed now—which helped me write a breath prayer. . . . I enjoy practicing breath prayer—'drilling down' into the texts/passages from Scripture. Finding that signature Scripture 'locked in' my breath prayer experience. I have more of the Word to hang the breath prayer onto." He continues to use breath prayers regularly and often.

Judith prefers the word *titles* to *names* when referring to this aspect of building a breath prayer. However, she often used the idea behind breath prayer—calling on God's attributes to meet our soul's deep need—in her daily devotions.

"Breath prayer," Stan wrote, "is a critically important part of all that API does. Constant refinement of the skill is necessary."

At the November seminar (the second class meeting of the year), Gretchen wrote, "This time around I was ready! It was exciting." Later in the year we had an assignment to come up with a breath prayer for a timeline. Gretchen wrote: "I really did it! Paid off with a breath prayer I feel will be a way to build myself—or be molded." On the end-of-year evaluation she responded that she used one or more breath prayers she developed at API very often and very often uses the names for God to fit the nature of a prayer. As part of her work in API Two, she taught breath prayer to the API One class.

Linda: "[Breath prayer] helps when I'm so stressed out I can't think straight enough to pray any other way! I'm still learning the names of God but how freeing to have so many to choose from." She wrote that she teared up as she prayed this elegant breath prayer: "Bread of Life, be all I need!" She and Phil have talked to their son about the power of breath prayers, and she would like to share it with more people.

Rick took a walk with his timeline breath prayer and had this to say about the experience: "Super amazing—for the first time, I see that God Our Righteousness is truly the one who kept me united with him and his family."

CHAPTER 6

PRAYING THE STORIES OF OUR LIVES

In the future, when your children ask you, "What do these stones mean?" tell them that the flow of the Jordan was cut off before the ark of the covenant of the LORD. When it crossed the Jordan, the waters of the Jordan were cut off. These stones are to be a memorial to the people of Israel forever.

—Josh. 4:6–7

I hope that by now you have experienced the value of praying breath prayer and lectio divina over the deep needs of your life. Isn't it refreshing to experience God in this way?

But there is more to the spiritual journey than dealing with the challenges and triumphs of the present moment. We are in the present moment precisely because we have passed through a long series of moments. God has been active in our lives, even before we were born, to bring us to this place in our journey, and he is intent on bringing us safe home to glory. For many, it has been a long and winding road. Our paths have taken us across gentle plains, over strenuous mountain passes, and down again into deep valleys. King David wrote of how the Lord led him into green pastures and quiet waters. But he also spoke of the Lord's presence with him in the darkest valleys of life (Ps. 23). Indeed, life in this world presents a multiplicity of high and lows. Sometimes, as in Job's case, the lows become long seasons of grief, hurt, and despair.

Our high points, on the other hand, can become such glorious events that, like the Apostle Paul's journey into the third heaven, we can barely speak of them (2 Corinthians 12). How we integrate these experiences into our lives determines a great deal about the health of our connection to the Lord. Scripture encourages us to remember the high points and low points of life and learn all we can from them. After all, the Lord has been there all along, guiding us into pathways of goodness and mercy.

In his book, *Pray Without Ceasing: Toward a Systematic Psychotheology of Christian Prayer Life*, Fabio Giardini focuses upon the benefits of "remembering God" and how such remembrances become a "springboard for prayer."[35] He encourages believers to remember what God has done in the past as part of our personal salvation history. Giardini points out how Scripture repeatedly exhorts God's people to contemplate God's saving purpose as revealed in their national history. Deuteronomy 8 is one such passage, teaching the people of God that when they arrive in the Promised Land, they must look back and recall all that the Lord has done for them. By meditating upon the past events of their lives, they would be in a position to incorporate the lessons of their history into the values they would live by in the land of promise. Moses warns them:

> When you have eaten and are satisfied, praise the LORD your God for the good land he has given you. Be careful that you *do not forget the LORD your God,* failing to observe his commands, his laws and his decrees that I am giving you this day. Otherwise, when you eat and are satisfied, when you build fine houses and settle down, and when your herds and flocks grow large and your silver and gold increase and all you have is multiplied, then your heart will become proud and you will forget the LORD your God, who brought you out of Egypt, out of the land of slavery. He led you through the vast and dreadful desert, that thirsty and waterless land, with its venomous snakes and scorpions. He brought you water out of hard rock. He gave you manna to eat in the desert,

something your fathers had never known, to humble and to test you so that in the end it might go well with you. You may say to yourself, "My power and the strength of my hands have produced this wealth for me." But *remember the LORD your God*, for it is he who gives you the ability to produce wealth, and so confirms his covenant, which he swore to your forefathers, as it is today.

—Deut. 8:10–18; italics mine

Moses exhorts the generation who would enter the Promised Land to remember what God had done for them during the long days of their childhood when they followed their parents through the desert wastes. Later, when they crossed over the Jordan River into the Promised Land, the Lord commanded them to place twelve stones at the water's edge as a reminder of the day that God stopped the flow of the river so the people could walk over on dry ground. Future generations would thus gain hope as they contemplated the past acts of God. They would be reminded of the greatness of God in history and would look with anticipation to his future works.

In the future, when your children ask you, "What do these stones mean?" tell them that the flow of the Jordan was cut off before the ark of the covenant of the LORD. When it crossed the Jordan, the waters of the Jordan were cut off. These stones are to be a memorial to the people of Israel forever.

—Josh. 4:6–7

Beginning with texts like these, Giardini reminds his readers that each believer individually has a salvation history. By remembering God's involvement in our life story, our prayer moves into a more familiar sphere as we open our heart to the God who has proven himself time and again as a trusted friend.[36]

Wonderful insights come when we think back on God's amazing choice to act as our friend! Jesus himself makes it clear that such friendship with God is a great springboard for prayer:

You are my friends if you do what I command. I no longer call you servants, because a servant does not know his master's business. Instead, I have called you friends, for everything that I learned from my Father I have made known to you. You did not choose me, but I chose you and appointed you so that you might go and bear fruit—fruit that will last—and so that whatever you ask in my name the Father will give you.

—John 15:14–16

In the psalms we see numerous examples of prayers that reflect on God's personal faithfulness through the challenges and triumphs of life. Psalm 34 is one such example. The superscript describes a humiliating situation in David's life that prompted his prayer:

Of David.

When he pretended to be insane before Abimelech, who drove him away, and he left.

What a low point! David resorts to acting like an insane person in order to escape from his enemy. But rising out of this shadowed time there is an opportunity for great praise. He voices words of high honor to the Lord when he reflects on that humbling event:

I will extol the LORD at all times;
his praise will always be on my lips.

My soul will boast in the LORD;
let the afflicted hear and rejoice.
Glorify the LORD with me;
let us exalt his name together.
I sought the LORD, and he answered me;
he delivered me from all my fears.
Those who look to him are radiant;
their faces are never covered with shame.

This poor man called, and the LORD heard him;
he saved him out of all his troubles.

—Ps. 34:1–6

What an encouragement!

Consider the many ups and downs in David's life. Ponder what it must have been like for him after he fled from Saul and hid away in the cave of Adullam with his band of outcasts and malcontents (1 Sam. 22:1–2). Perhaps he might have thought to himself, "If I am supposed to be king, what am I doing here?" Imagine David thinking back to his anointing by Samuel, his triumph over Goliath, his appointment as a commander in King Saul's army, and his marriage to the king's daughter. What great times! But then King Saul, his own father-in-law, viciously turns against him, trying to spear him to the wall. Now he has made his escape. As he ponders these high points and low points of his life, what lessons would he focus upon? Would he recognize that through all of these difficult events that God was preparing him to be a great king? Scripture makes it clear that it was God's inspired plan to prepare a shepherd boy to become a shepherd king to guide his people Israel:

> He chose David his servant
> and took him from the sheep pens;
> from tending the sheep he brought him
> to be the shepherd of his people Jacob,
> of Israel his inheritance.
> And David shepherded them with integrity of heart;
> with skillful hands he led them.
>
> —Ps. 78:70–72

The God who brought David from a life as a shepherd boy to the kingship of a nation is the God we can trust to work out his purposes in the low points and high points of our lives.[37]

In the New Testament, Paul invites believers to consider how God has been at work in the events of their lives. He writes to the Philippians, reminding them of the personal history that they share. Paul assures them that just as God has been faithfully at work in their past, so also he will be faithfully working in their future:

> I thank my God every time I remember you. In all my prayers for all of you, I always pray with joy because of your partnership

in the gospel from the first day until now, being confident of
this, that he who began a good work in you will carry it on to
completion until the day of Christ Jesus.

—Phil. 1:3–6

Paul is encouraging the believers in Philippi to think back
over the events that brought the Gospel to their city and gave
them new birth in Christ. Lydia, the first woman saved, the jailor
and his family, and all of the other believers would remember the
astounding events that brought them to Christ. But they would
also remember the severe beating Paul and Silas endured and the
suffering that had come into their lives for the sake of Christ (Acts
16). As they pondered these high points and low points in light
of God's sovereign actions, they would be encouraged to continue
their partnership in the gospel. They could be confident that God
would be faithful to bring glory to himself even through the troubles
that were sure to come.

Other New Testament writers urge us to consider the events of
the past. The writer to the Hebrews calls his readers to think about
the leaders God had given them over the course of their lives and
model their lives accordingly:

Remember your leaders, who spoke the word of God to you.
Consider the outcome of their way of life and imitate their faith.
Jesus Christ is the same yesterday and today and forever.

—Heb.13:7–8

As we remember those leaders God used to influence our lives,
we can recall the lessons and insights that they brought us. As we
consider the outcome of their way of life, we are increasingly able
to give thanks for the grace God has shown in the past and look
forward in hope to the good things God will do in the future.[38]

In the book of Revelation, the Lord Jesus Christ urges the church
at Ephesus to look back and take stock of how far they have fallen
and return to the active love they once demonstrated for him:

Yet I hold this against you: You have forsaken your first love.
Remember the height from which you have fallen! Repent and
do the things you did at first. If you do not repent, I will come
to you and remove your lampstand from its place.

—Rev. 2:4–5

The Lord is calling the members of the Ephesian church to
remember the wonders of their previous experience in Christ. And
he is asking them to evaluate the low point in which they currently
find themselves. Through meditating and praying over the heights
of their journey with Jesus, they will be reminded of how God
has faithfully been working through faith and love to bring them
through the depths. This memory will stimulate them to rise up
from their current situation and "do the things you did at first,"
thus renewing their love for the Lord.

We do well to remember the high points of our spiritual journey
and the times when we especially experienced the love Jesus has
poured out upon us. Then if there are things we must change so
that we may return to our first love, we may make every effort to
do so. By prayerfully remembering our past and offering the events
of our lives up to the Lord, we gain a greater appreciation for God's
goodness and the grace he shows in calling us his friends. We gain
insight into how he has been seeking to form us into the likeness
of his Son. We gain a deeper sense of thankfulness as we better
understand how God has been present in the high points and low
points of our lives.

But what does it look like when people pray in this way? Let
me share some examples with you.

Jehovah Nissi, Fulfill Your Calling in our Lives

This moment for my wife Kathryn and me came to be known as
the hug. The year was 1984. I had just walked the aisle at graduation
from seminary, and there was my devoted wife, ready to sweep me
up in her arms. What a banner moment! After four long years of
preparing to preach, I was finally graduating. During my teen years,
God had made his calling clear, and now the academic training was

complete. But where would we go to fulfill that calling? And more importantly, could I do it? Could I actually preach God's Word in such a way that would sustain the life of a congregation through the manifold challenges of life? I needed assurance that God was going to put us to work for him, and I needed confidence to believe that this work we would do would matter.

With the perspective of a more than a quarter-century in the pastorate, I took a look back at what I needed most from God at that moment of triumph that was shadowed by uncertainty. I was drawn to the name, Jehovah Nissi, the Lord My Banner. I read the story in Exodus 17:8–16, where Moses stood upon the mountain above the battlefield with the staff of God in his hands. As Moses held up the symbol of God's mighty deliverance, the Israelites prevailed in battle. Aaron and Hur stood by his side, holding up his weakening hands. After the battle was won, Moses built an altar and named it, "The Lord My Banner." And he said, "For hands were lifted up to the throne of the LORD." God had been a banner of victory for the nation. He had not called them to be defeated—he had called them to prevail. And so my breath prayer coming out of this Scripture became, Jehovah Nissi, fulfill your calling in my life.

As I prayed lectio divina upon this passage, I began to consider all of the people who had held up our hands in ministry since that first pastorate began in 1984. I remembered how as we were graduating and wondering where we would be going, members of that first church were praying for us. Though they did not know our names, God was holding up our arms through their prayers. And their prayers saw us through eight eventful years in which God honed that gift and call to preach. As I meditated on Exodus 17, I saw that members of God's army had indeed looked to the Lord through my preaching and teaching and gained courage to fight on one more day. Even through all the struggles, God was using me as I stood before his people week after week, with the Word of God in my hands, the source and symbol of their victory.

But how has this worked out in the lives of others?

After praying over events from his past, Ryan Jensema, Senior Pastor of Northwest Baptist Church in Bellingham, Washington wrote: "Praying your timeline—this one amazed me. At first I didn't think delving into the past and identifying past needs would have any value. As I did it, I found God's work in my life to overwhelm me all over again. I appreciated and loved God more for how he worked things out now. I also love how the lectio and breath prayer tie into this step so that God's work is seen in my life. It was so rich and nurturing, even though it touched on some painful memories."

Aaron was another person who benefitted greatly by prayerfully pondering past events. He was a high-energy seminarian, self-described "aggressive apprentice," and an effective mentor of men. After being introduced to lectio divina and breath prayer, he began to apply the skills to unsettling memories of past sins. He felt the need to "detect and cut out the ugly baggage of my soul" lest he infect those he leads. He chose Psalm 51 for meditation and upon reflection, created two breath prayers arising from the psalm. His first prayer was "Yahweh Shalom, God of Peace, help me feel as clean as you have made me." He yearned for the deep peace that comes through being clean before God. His second prayer was "Yahweh Tsidkenu, God of Righteousness, send me to share your righteousness." This prayer expressed his desire to share the Word of God with integrity and without shame. The second breath prayer grew out of Psalm 51:12–13, "Restore to me the joy of your salvation and grant me a willing spirit, to sustain me. Then I will teach transgressors your ways, and sinners will turn back to you."

Commenting on the value of his breath prayers, Aaron compared them to a link on a webpage: "Breath prayer becomes a link—you click on it and it opens up a window to a conversation with God."

At a later date, Aaron expanded on this metaphor: "The breath prayer was a catalyst to launch the extended time in prayer that I truly need. It was a summary, opening the conversation with a thematic emphasis." Aaron describes the results of his prayer: "The eternal is that he has made me clean. The temporal is that I feel it in me. He makes me feel more and more free from past uncleanliness."

In order to further assure the deep cleansing he desired, Aaron sought insight from a counselor on the staff of the seminary. After discussing the grace that he was experiencing through the breath prayer and lectio divina on Psalm 51, the counselor asked if Aaron would be willing to share his experiences with the seminary student body in a fall chapel service. Aaron agreed. After his chapel testimony, Aaron wrote to report: "I'm told by counselors in Student Services that it had the desired effect of helping others to have the courage to come forward too. Praise the Lord."

API Participants Respond

Judith gave the timeline exercise a high mark at the February seminar, "Because it helps organize places I need to revisit and bring to spiritual resolution."

Charles: "I understand that timelines are a wonderful idea. But I always have trouble sorting wheat from chaff in what to include." But he adds, "I did an extensive life review for several months which resulted in a 'faith choice' you wouldn't believe. It changed my perspective of both my life and the faithfulness of God."

Gretchen: "I believe as we change, the process gets better and opens our hearts more. I really worked on my timeline breath prayer. [It] came to me between Psalm 139 and the Potter's passage, Jeremiah 18:1–6: God made me to be wonderful. As I am I in the world . . . he is there to mold and maintain his wonderful creation. . . . This molding is soothing like a potter's moist hands."

For Marlee, the reflecting time on Psalm 139 leading up to our timeline was, "Absolutely profound. I had so been set up for this over the month with breath prayer and a book I am reading on creativity. I will be praying through these ten years—because how God showed up was such a profound revelation. My breath prayer came right to the surface."

Rick: "Creating a timeline—even as a retired guy was great and very insightful. This is my first time doing this—it is very helpful to see the big picture! I realize who has been there through the highs and lows."

Phil says he has pondered his timeline often since creating it. During his second year, he led the API One class through timeline creation. He summarized the value of timeline saying, "Whatever comes in life, I will go through it with God."

Linda: "What I liked about timeline creation was the introspection. I think about my past a lot, so it was a good outlet. Since creating my timeline, I've thought more about what God has done there."

Robin received insight on the long look at life from reading Frank Laubach's, *Letters by a Modern Mystic*.[39] "I am realizing how I can be impulsive and act out of my own will without waiting to see if it is what God wants me to do. Then I am stressed out and overwhelmed because I have stepped out of his will, even in doing good, or in doing ministry. But God brings the opportunities and we don't need to feel overwhelmed because he provides all we need for what he wants us to do."

Dave wrote that creating his timeline was "a bit of a struggle," but he persisted. Later he said, "Exploring low and high points though difficult, was very beneficial. [It helped to use] breath prayers and signature Scripture. My soul friend had wonderful insight." Dave reports that he has looked back and pondered his timeline many times.

Ken reflected deeply on the results of praying our stories. He said he learned best by the example set by Pastor Wes as he shared so much about his own life. "He (Wes) learned to use these very same tools as God walked him through the valleys and mountaintops he experienced. He was describing relationship." And then later he said, "It is good to reflect on God's faithfulness throughout my career and life. Praise God!"

Karen: "This is a very important exercise. It doesn't just happen once. Your timeline should be revisited now and then. The Holy Spirit may bring things to your attention that you haven't resolved yet. It is important to remember that God has been with you through all the highs and lows. It helps to remind us of God's great love for us. A heart of thankfulness is the fruit of this work."

Stan: "[The timeline creation exercise] was not as scary as I feared it would be. It was illuminating to see it all fall out onto a linear diagram; that's now how I am used to viewing key points."

Praying the Stories of Our Lives

Let's move now toward praying over selected events from our personal timeline. God has been at work all along to develop us into the image of Christ. He has taken us through highs and lows. As we prayerfully reflect upon these events, we gain insight into how the Lord has been working. By praying over these key moments in his shaping process, we gain insight into how God has equipped us to meet the challenges of today. If we are honest, we will see that in some cases, he has more work to do in healing us and shaping us.

Take some time to construct a simple, twenty-point timeline of your life. Using an 8 x 10 piece of paper, draw a horizontal line across the page, leaving space above and below the line to plot the high points and low points of your journey. As you mark the highs and lows, consider the people, the places and the events that have influenced the course of your life.

For high points, consider the celebrations of your life—events when life opened up before you—such as your salvation, a spiritual victory, a graduation, a wedding, the birth of a child, a call to ministry, an accomplishment you always dreamed of doing. For low points, consider when you experienced a time of grief or loss, when you were impacted by your own sins or those of another person, when a time of personal failure led you deeper into the grace of God, or when you were humbled by sickness or sorrow.

For instance, in the life of David, his timeline might start to look something like this:

A Timeline of David's Early Years

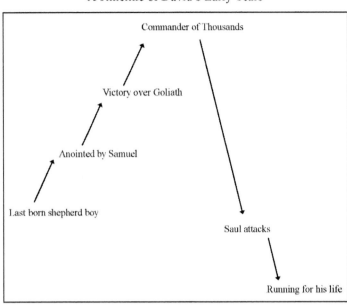

As you consider the low points of your journey, take time to pray lectio divina on Paul's reflections concerning a difficult time in his life journey as recorded in 2 Corinthians 1:3–11. As you pray, consider how the power of the resurrection brought Paul through the depths and into the healing presence of the Lord.

As you conclude your lectio, read James 1:1–12. Thank God for the power he has given you to persevere through challenging circumstances. Take a moment to consider the wisdom you have gained from the Lord through these trials and tests.

As you conclude your meditations, consider afresh God's promises to work in your life for his good purpose. Spend some time praying over your timeline, rejoicing in God's unshakeable promise that he will complete what he began when he envisioned your birth, the time of your re-birth, and your final destination with him safe home in glory. With this in mind, prayerfully select two events from your timeline: a high point and a low point. Briefly summarize these events in your journal. In the next chapters, we'll provide the opportunity for you to begin praying breath prayer and lectio over the events of your life.

CHAPTER 7

PRAYING OUR LOW POINTS

HOW TO RECEIVE CARE FROM GOD'S CHARACTER

For just as the sufferings of Christ flow over into our lives, so also through Christ our comfort overflows.

—2 Cor. 1:5

Father of Compassion, grant us passion to thrive in our brokenness.

June 13, 2006—Not since the Cowardly Lion has an animal's appearance been so at odds with its attitude. On June 4 a black bear wandered into a West Milford, New Jersey, back yard, was confronted by a 15-pound tabby cat . . . and fled up a neighbor's tree. Hissing at the base of the tree, Jack the clawless cat kept the bear at bay for about 15 minutes, and then ran him up another tree after an attempted escape. Finally, Jack's owner, Donna Dickey, called the cat inside, and the timorous trespasser disappeared back into the woods. "He doesn't want anybody in his yard," Dickey said of Jack in an interview with the Newark *Star Ledger*. Full-grown black bears weigh between 200 and 600 pounds and measure as much as 6 feet (1.8 meters) long. Their diets can include fruits, honey, insects, acorns and animals as big as moose calves—a fact apparently lost on Jack.[40]

85

And a fact lost on that bear!

We all encounter many troubles on our life's journey. Whether we are like the cat or the bear in this story, we often have our hands full. Oh, to have the courage of that cat. But think about the bear. That would certainly not qualify as one of the high points of his life story! I'm sure he would not want to talk about it with his bear buddies back in the deep woods.

In the same way, we encounter events in life that reveal our weakness, our vulnerability and our need. Often they confuse us, and like the bear, we head up our tree and just stay up there until the perceived danger passes. Sometimes we stay longer than necessary, or we slink back down and head for what we hope is a safe place. Most of the time, we'd rather not talk about it. But it is precisely those times when we can experience the grace of God most profoundly. Jesus said we would have trouble in this world. And we do. Perhaps you can identify a long list of problems that have the potential to overwhelm your life. But praying through them gives us a strong sense of God's continued presence. Even in the lowest times, and perhaps most in the lowest times, we become deeply aware of God's guiding presence.

Often it is hard to see what he is doing in these low moments because our vision is blurred by tears. Our perceptions are clouded by grief that may lead us to anger, which if left to fester, leads to bitterness. Sometimes the only thing we can see is our own wounded self—isolated in the darkness of our overwhelming problem. We wonder where God is. We doubt that he is up to any good at all. But as we reflect and look back with the eyes of faith upon past low times, we are increasingly able to see more of what God was doing. We may begin to see what he still wants to do and continues to say to us through them. We begin to discern that he was there, guiding us, and providing what we most needed. As a result, we gain confidence for our current situation, and look with hope upon our future.

Take a few moments now and prayerfully read Paul's reflection of a low time in his life, and how he experienced the profound comfort of the Lord. Think about the core ideas of this passage. Consider the main message and how the verses fit together.

Praise be to the God and Father of our Lord Jesus Christ, the Father of compassion and the God of all comfort, who comforts us in all our troubles, so that we can comfort those in any trouble with the comfort we ourselves have received from God. For just as the sufferings of Christ flow over into our lives, so also through Christ our comfort overflows. If we are distressed, it is for your comfort and salvation; if we are comforted, it is for your comfort, which produces in you patient endurance of the same sufferings we suffer. And our hope for you is firm, because we know that just as you share in our sufferings, so also you share in our comfort.
—2 Cor. 1:3–7

The first chapter in 2 Corinthians is all about a low time in the life of God's anointed missionary, Paul the apostle. The next few verses tell how Paul went through a time so troubled that he says he felt the sentence of death within himself. He figured this was the end of the line for him. We are not told exactly what the crisis was, and perhaps that's better for us. Rather than focusing on the particular problem—a problem we might not be able to relate to—Paul journals about the comfort he experienced. He writes about the strength of the comfort that found him in the depth of his distress. He looks back on one of the lowest moments of his life and praises the Lord. We can do the same.

Our Comfort Overflows

My wife, Kathryn, and I would like to share with you one of those low seasons of our life and how God met us there. As Kathryn and I share our story, we'd like to invite you to look back on your own story. We want to encourage you to listen to God about a time in your life that you may most desire to forget. As you do, we are confident that God will meet you with grace in your point of pain and deepen your experience of his comfort.

Six weeks after we married, Kathryn and I moved to Dallas, Texas, where I was enrolled in seminary. The plan was for her to teach school during the four years I studied and then leave the classroom to be a homemaker and mother. As seminary graduation approached, we decided it might be prudent to wait another year until I was settled in the pastorate before we started a family. But two years later, we began to realize that our careful planning did not mean we were in control. What was so simple and automatic for most couples—conceiving a child—proved to be incredibly difficult for us. After working with several doctors and spending thousands of dollars, we were no closer to bringing a child into this world. We looked into adoption and were stymied by the inch-thick stack of paperwork, the legacy of disappointment from our medical efforts, and the even-more-thousands of dollars required. Though we did not understand God's purpose and even felt abandoned by God in this struggle, he met us along the path, and eventually released us from this quest. God did not grant us a child of our own, and the pain of that loss lingers a quarter-century later. But as life has unfolded, we're thankful for the blessings God has sent in other ways.

When I launched this project on experiencing the grace of God where we need it most, I knew that I wanted to immerse this most painful time in our lives in the healing presence of God. I wanted to pray more deeply over this season of our lives because I felt that God had additional things to say to us about it. In March of 2006, I was leading a reflective prayer retreat at the beautiful Methow Valley Ranch and had designed the retreat for each participant to pray over a low point in their lives. On that low-point day, I chose to immerse myself once more in the difficult reality of our childlessness.

After the morning session, I went to my room with my Bible, my journal, and a box of Kleenex for this appointment with the Lord. I didn't yet have a breath prayer for this need, and I was not sure of the name of God I wanted to use. But I knew I wanted to immerse myself in 2 Corinthians 1 where Paul speaks of the comfort and compassion of the Lord. I prayed, wept, meditated on 2 Corinthians 1:3–7, wrote in my journal, soaked in a hot bath, and emerged with a bright sense of renewal and deep thanks. This experience deepened some transformational truths which emerged from this Scripture text.

Our Troubles Flow Deep . . . God's Comfort Flows Deeper Still

. . . so also through Christ our comfort overflows.

I saw that God's comfort flows over, around, and through our grief. Kathryn and I have learned some things about grief on this road. I remember an evening at our home in Hoquiam, Washington, when Kathryn came back with a doctor's report that revealed the depth of our medical problems. That evening I wept like I'd never wept before. It was one of those scary events where you get tingling in your hands—too much weeping and not enough breathing! It's the kind of event you don't want to revisit.

But at the retreat as I encountered that old grief once again, I felt wrapped up in the warm presence of the Lord. No desperate weeping. No buzzing hands and fingertips. There were tears, yes, but instead of a sense of losing control, I felt surrounded by the warmth of God's comfort. Like the warmth of that winter comforter on the bed, God's healing presence kept me safe. The tears flowed, but I wasn't swept away in the flood. Instead, I received precious new insights into the character of God and what he had done and was doing in our lives through our childlessness. In that prayer time, I saw that through Christ our comfort overflows. I saw how Christ, the eternal, risen, reigning Lord is the overwhelming source of comfort. Never running short, he provides a super-abundance of comfort for all who seek him. He provides hope for the most broken. As I prayed over this passage, I saw again how God had met us in our grief, and how he had provided such a gracious supply of comfort.

How Did God's Comfort Overflow Our Grief?

First, he comforted us through a prayer of the heart. Kathryn and I had spent ourselves financially, emotionally, and spiritually in our efforts to conceive. But after several medical interventions, we were childless still. The pain, disappointment and anger were deep. During a solo trip to the infertility clinic ninety miles from home, Kathryn had a profound encounter with God. The core of his message was that childlessness was our refining fire, and he was lovingly purifying us for his own glory. She sensed that we were at the end of this path, but she told the Lord that if he wanted us to cease treatments, that he would have to tell me. So she began praying through the rest of the summer that God would tell her husband that it was time to stop the medical treatments. Since God did not answer immediately, we went through one more round of procedures. Kathryn was not surprised when it was clear that this was also a fruitless effort, and she continued to trust God to speak to me.

Second, God comforted us through hearing his voice. That September, I was at a men's retreat when the Lord answered Kathryn's prayer. It was during a worship time which was focused on servanthood. We were standing in worship when I clearly heard the Lord speak, "Will you be childless for me?" In his grace, he repeated his question, "Will you be childless for me?" I immediately replied, "Yes, Lord, for you, but not for anyone else." That was something only the Lord could ask. And I felt assured that he had a good reason and that there would be a calling to something else in our lives.

But then he deepened our comfort through the gift of double confirmation. I went home from the weekend retreat, and on Monday afternoon, Kathryn and I took a long walk on a wide beach on the pounding Pacific Ocean. I told her what the Lord had asked of me. That's when she shared that over the course of the summer she had been praying that God would speak to me about our situation, and had, in fact, been walking in the neighborhood praying that prayer during the evening when I had heard the Lord so clearly. We took that as a double confirmation and felt immediately released from our efforts to become parents.

Double confirmation is a means that God uses to underscore his leadership in our lives. He does this repeatedly in Scripture. For instance, when God called Abram, he communicated not once, but twice (Genesis 12 and 15). When the Lord let Joseph know that he was going to rule over his brothers, he gave him not one dream but two. When the angel told Mary that she would conceive and bear a Son, he also told Joseph. Then, just for good measure, he told Mary's cousin, Elizabeth, as well. You get the idea.

Through double confirmation, God had made it clear to us that we would be childless, and that by doing so we would be fulfilling a calling from him. As we took this step, the anger began to subside. Later that fall, Kathryn attended a women's retreat at the same venue where I had heard from God. While there, one of the worship leaders told her personal story of God's miraculous provision of a child after a season of infertility. Kathryn felt moved to abruptly get up and leave the meeting, the familiar heart-pounding grief and disillusionment welling up inside her. But where previously the pain and anger would have been too much to bear, she knew, "This time I was running to God for comfort, rather than away from him."

How had God comforted us? First, he led Kathryn to pray a deep prayer of the heart. In obedience, Kathryn prayed until I heard the call. God asked me . . . twice. He confirmed his calling to each of us. We knew we had heard from God.

Comfort Overflows

Our comfort began to overflow when the Lord opened the way for us to host the daughter of good friends who had moved away to a small town in Eastern Washington. The family moved at the start of Julie's senior year of high school, exiling her far from the friends she'd grown up with and her close-knit school peers. After a heart felt conversation with her dad, we made arrangements for Julie to come to live with us. Over the next two and half years, while she finished high school and community college, she brought joy and healing to our home.

Through Julie, Jesus brought fresh life into our home. She brought us out of ourselves, out of our private pain and into a wider world. Her laughter, music, and beauty won us over. She expanded our Christian fellowship, filling our home with her friends. Her creative and unpredictable boyfriend, Sam (who is now her husband), kept us entertained. He loved music, people, and God and was always coming up with something new. His hunger for God and his passion to grow refreshed us. Julie and Sam helped us pick out our dog, Henry. We had a great time together. Comfort overflowed. To this day, our lives are richer because of Julie and

Sam Brueher.[41] Years later when I prayed over this period of our lives, I became increasingly thankful for how God led the way out of that season of struggle. This breath prayer flowed out: *Father of compassion, grant us passion to thrive in our brokenness.*

So let me encourage you to make a date with God and do some work on a difficult season in your life. Let God take you back and show you what he was up to in that challenging time. Let the deeper lessons emerge; listen for his calling.

Distress Carries a High Purpose

I continued to pray over 2 Corinthians 1:3–7 for the next few weeks after the prayer retreat. Another line in Paul's litany of comfort made an impression on me: "If we are distressed, it is for your comfort . . ."

Processing our pain through God's healing presence leads us to care for and comfort others. We become comforters by being comforted by God. As I prayed over these verses, I saw more deeply how our distress created a way to bring comfort to Julie. She had been sad, withdrawn, and depressed in her new home. She was missing Sam, she was missing her friends, and she was missing out on her final year with the classmates she had gone to school with since kindergarten. But back in town with us, she came alive again. She entered the Miss Grays Harbor beauty pageant and won the Miss Congeniality award. Kathryn helped her with costuming and rehearsals for her performance. We had a blast! The comfort that flowed to us flowed through us, and blessed Julie and Sam. Our pain translated into gain for them both. There was purpose in our distress.

Praying over this passage for a few weeks deepened my sense of God's healing grace, increased my joy, and called me into a greater purpose for our lives. Months later I returned and prayed lectio over it again. This time I thought about the second young woman God sent us, who lived in our home, and who became like a daughter to us: Jessica.

Comfort Overflows, Again!

Jessica came into our lives through a young adults group that we hosted in our home. She eventually came to live with us and became like a second daughter. As I prayed over 2 Corinthians 1 once more, God brought new meaning to our years of distress when I realized that during those same years, Jessica was also in great distress. While we were going through our frustrating attempts to conceive, Jessica was a young girl growing up in a very difficult family situation. While we were in pain, she was in pain. When we encountered Christ for our healing, he was also there for her. He led her to himself and into a wonderful church family. In her early twenties, God brought her into our home, and comfort overflowed. In healing her, the Father of Compassion was healing us. We will tell more of her story in the next chapter, about how God was at work during one of the highest moments in our life. By praying over this same passage with Jessica in mind, I saw that our sufferings prepared a place for her in our family. This brought new meaning to those years of pain.

Our distress . . . led us to the comfort that flows from Christ.

Jessica's distress . . . led her to the comfort that flows from Christ.

The Father of Compassion brought us together . . . and comfort overflowed.

Grace to Comfort Others

One of the ways that pain works is that it focuses our attention on the deep need in our life. But the pain only gets worse if we keep our focus upon our needs, our wants, or our desires. Pain has the grave potential to lead us into despair if we isolate our attention onto the sadness of our own souls. Another way to say this is that pain has a way of getting us stuck on our hurting selves. We become full of ourselves. Some wise person said that he who is wrapped up in himself makes a very small package indeed. When our hearts are full of ourselves, the way God heals us is to break our hearts. C. S. Lewis celebrated that breaking in a poem called, "As the Ruin Falls."[42] Phil Keaggy set Lewis' poem to music, and

93

I've been listening to it for years.[43] In the poem, Lewis laments the self-centered ruin that was his life. His life is falling apart, and the poet's heart is breaking. For this, Lewis gives thanks. He blesses the Lord for bringing his ruined heart into a place where his pains have become precious. Why do they become precious? The pains God gives become precious when they empty us of ourselves. As we are emptied of ourselves, God comes to fill that hollowed out space within. He moves toward us with his comfort. He gently fills us with himself. We experience his compassion, and as his comfort overflows in our lives, he moves us out to his greater purpose in the world. He moves us to fix our attention on others. We abandon our mercenary, self-seeking ways and instead become missionaries of peace.

Here's a small test. Ask yourself: "To what extent am I able to comfort others?" If you are honest, perhaps your answer is "not much," or "I just don't seem to be able to connect like that," or "there's too much going on with me to give much attention to anyone else." If this is true, then ask yourself, "Where do I most need the healing grace of God in my life?" I want to encourage you to immerse your soul in the mercy of God. When you do, you will experience hope that is contagious.

We Gain Hope for Others

Another line of Paul's testimony became powerful for me:

And our hope for you is firm, because we know that just as you share in our sufferings, so also you share in our comfort.

—2 Cor. 1:7

Because of what Jesus did for Kathryn and me, and for Julie and Jessica, we have great confidence that he will be there for you too. We are all going to be okay. The Father of the Fatherless is watching out for you. The Father of Compassion is intent on immersing you in his love.

During this process of praying over a low point, a breath prayer began to emerge: "Father of mercies, grant me courage to embrace my brokenness."

Rather than run from my brokenness, I prayed, Lord give me courage to serve and lead out of my brokenness. As I prayed over this, I understood how I have devoted great energy to launch campaigns and work on projects that are secret attempts on my part to deny my brokenness. So I began to pray, "Lord, grant me passion and courage to thrive in brokenness. Give me strength to lead in brokenness."

Now we pray, *"Father of Compassion, grant us passion to thrive our brokenness. Father, let us not just survive, not just get by, but let us thrive. Lord, make this deep ache a place from which we are able to flourish, develop and grow strong. Fulfill your calling in our lives. Connect us deeply to a world in pain; allow us to be a means by which your comfort overflows. Through Jesus we pray, Amen."* By answering this prayer of the heart, God fulfilled a calling that he had placed upon us. We have learned the truth that, as C. S. Lewis has said, God... "shouts in our pain."[44] We have learned that through pain, God connects us deeply with the world, and through that connection, God's comfort overflows.

Action Steps

1. Take time to consider a low point in your life. You may want to make an appointment with God to ponder this challenging time. Ask yourself the following questions:

   What did I need most from God at that time?
   What name of God best corresponds to my soul's need in that season of life?
   What would have been an appropriate breath prayer for that season?

2. Make a date with God to pray over your low point.

   Chose a key Scripture that reveals that God is good at meeting your kind of need.
   Set aside private, secure time to meet with God.
   Pray over your selected passage.

Journal your prayers, insights and reflections.
Seek the insights of a mature, compassionate friend in Christ.

3. Keep praying over your low point.

   Continue to pray your low point breath prayer.
   Over the next several days, return to your passage for prayer and meditation.
   Continue to gain counsel from a trusted spiritual friend.

In the next chapter, we will move to meditating on a high point in our life. Remember, the Lord shouts to us in our pains, and he whispers to us in our pleasures. Listen carefully to what God is speaking to you in the troubles of your life.

API Participants Respond

Michael Card's, *Sacred Sorrow Experience Guide: Reaching Out to God in the Lost Language of Lament* is one of the books we read during the API academic year. It is an excellent and sympathetic companion for us as we go through a low-point journey. Here are a few folks' reactions to the book.

Robin: "It is truly though lament that we come close to God. We come to love him for his loving-kindness and presence instead of only loving him for what he can do for us. When trials come our way or God does not answer our prayers the way we think he should . . . it causes us to wrestle with him, wrestle until we have spent ourselves and are left with just him. The Holy Spirit pointed out to me as I read this book that I have been putting my hope in my circumstances, not God. I realize that the Scriptures I have run to in desperation and dwelt upon as I seek God to help me, are the ones that really have taken root."

Karen: "When I was going through cancer treatments, there were many nights when sleep escaped me. I would sit up in bed and read the Psalms. I continued reading through the Psalms month after month. *Sacred Sorrow* reminded me of that practice. What I found was that the psalmist would pour out his heart to the Lord, then there would be a *but* or a *yet* . . . I did not know that it was a *vav adversative* (a technical grammatical term indicating the writer's change of heart which is a key feature of lament literature), but I did notice a change in the psalmist's thinking. It was these *buts* and *yets* that I hung on to. The words *but God* or *yet God* stood out to me. It is OK to lament as long as it takes you back to God, to his character and what he has done in the past."

Another way API teaches low-point processing is to provide a safe place to talk about things we'd rather keep hidden away. Here are a few comments about praying though low-points on retreat.

Dave: "Timeline was a struggle—especially revisiting the low points. But I could see where God has been with me through the low points. Discussing our reflections was quite meaningful."

In April of 2013, Linda was blunt: "Revisiting my low point was hard. I felt distractible and not wanting to go there. Low point stuff hurts!" Later she said, "I dreaded this, and yet it was so revelatory and necessary." By January of 2014 she reported, "[The low point sharing was] such a sweet work of God: healthy and healing. What a wonderful, structured exercise!"

Watching the Disney film, *The Kid* provided a safe way for Rick to share about low points. "Russ (the main character) was the perfect jerk (reminds me of me). I continue to apply what I learned about connections and being united with the Trinity, with my sweetheart, and how he has transformed my heart in all my relationships."

Phil admitted that he doesn't want to do these exercises, but that he usually ends up enjoying them. "It is *needed*." In the group, he added, there was "warm fellowship and honest sharing—it was a safe place."

Ken: "My low point has always frozen me and kept me from moving forward. I need to keep my eyes on Jesus. I know where Jesus is . . . He is in me. He is always with me."

Judith: "In a general way everything that helps us to know the depths of another person's heart is positive even if what they share is a downer for them. . . . [In my own life] there are too many loose ends—I need to close the circle on some events. . . . I see tremendous future usefulness for this. . . . I've been using [stealth soul friendship praying] in classes at school [to deal with the after-effects of these student's low points]. . . . It works—'light comes into the world and darkness has not overcome it.'" Summarizing how low points are transformed into the highest of high points she wrote, "I see that he always had my back. I need to multiply that certainty and release like a million, million doves."

Marlee caught the essence of low-point processing when she reflected on how she put it to work in her life coaching role. While listening to another woman share about a difficult situation at work, Marlee said, "I felt so helpless—praying continuously." But then she experienced what so often happens: a low point turns into a high point because God, amazingly, unexpectedly, meets us there. "I sensed the Lord met [this woman] through our conversation."

Processing low points through discussion in a caring group, Stan said, was "most helpful in alleviating any sense of isolation in the struggles common to so many. Often, the thoughts shared by others were apropos to my own experience."

Charles named the small group discussions as the most meaningful part of a long day praying over low points on the second retreat. He said he received an encouraging change of direction. In fact, he said it went "beyond my greatest hope—I am still in awe." In addition, he found an inspired voice to minister to others in their need.

Gretchen went into the Praying Our Challenges and Triumphs retreat apprehensive about the negative human emotions that might disrupt the difficult work of praying over low points. Her fear was hugely relieved: "God has been showing me to keep my eyes on Jesus. . . . The small group allows us to open up." Her name for God in her timeline breath prayer was Emmanuel—God is with us!

CHAPTER 8

PRAYING OUR HIGH POINTS

HOW TO RECEIVE CARE FROM GOD'S CHARACTER

I know a man in Christ who fourteen years ago was caught up to the third heaven. Whether it was in the body or out of the body I do not know—God knows. And I know that this man—whether in the body or apart from the body I do not know, but God knows— was caught up to paradise and heard inexpressible things, things that no one is permitted to tell.
—2 Cor. 12:2–4

Remember the story of Jack, the fifteen-pound cat who chased a two hundred-pound black bear up a tree—not once, but twice? His courageous exploits got him written up in the local paper! (See chapter 7). While this must have been an embarrassing low point for the bear, for Jack, it was a high moment in his little cat life. From that day on, that tabby had bragging rights to the whole neighborhood!

In the last chapter, Kathryn and I shared how God led us through one of the lowest seasons of our lives. We are increasingly thankful for the good work the Lord did and for how he revealed himself to us at that time. We emerged broken, yet with thankful hearts. With C. S. Lewis we can celebrate our pains as gifts from God.[45]

Through praying our Father of Compassion breath prayer, (Father of Compassion, grant us passion to thrive in our broken-ness), God has increased his healing grace in our lives. He has given us grace to comfort those who are in many troubles with the comfort we ourselves have received from God. There are a myriad of pain sources in this world, but God's comfort is like light flowing through a great prism—the beauty of his healing is able to shine upon every pain. There is an overwhelming, superabundance of comfort that flows from Christ, and if you have tasted the comfort of Jesus, you know that there is hope for anybody.

But breath prayer and lectio are more than tools of healing for the low points in our lives. They are also tools for celebration. It is easy to forget that in the high moments of our lives, God is still shaping us for his work in the world. Reflecting on these times also yields rich results. They lead us to celebrate, give thanks, and to look forward in hope.

As I continued to develop and pray over my timeline, one of the moments that I was eager to pray about was the day I gave Jessica away in marriage. The wedding took place in a grassy park in Niagara-on-the-Lake, Ontario. I would be on her right and her birth-father on her left as she went forward to meet her groom.

A little back-story here: when Jessica was eighteen months old, her father went to prison for his part in a violent crime. He was incarcerated until she was twelve years old, but because she lived in Washington and he lived in Oregon, the conditions of his parole dictated that he could not cross state lines to visit her. During those growing up years, no one told her why her father was absent. It wasn't until she was seventeen years old that she learned that her dad had been involved in a crime where someone was killed and that he had gone to prison. Imagine the shock! When she was twenty years old, she finally met her father.

During those years there had been other step-dads. None of these men were good news to her. Rather than gain comfort, strength, and wisdom from them, she learned to get out of harm's way. She did not have a mature man in her life who showed her compassion, kindness, or love. She found those precious gifts in the Lord Jesus; she found them in her pastor, and in her early 20s, she found them in me.

Jessica had become a part of a college and career fellowship group that Kathryn and I were hosting in our home. Jessica's pastor and my good friend, Bruce Ingram, had a vision for a network of small groups between the smaller churches of our city. We loved the idea, so we launched a group that eventually involved young people from a number of area churches. Jessica came to the second meeting where she nervously sat on the floor next to her best friend. The group became a close fellowship of dedicated Christian young people.

Jessica came to housesit for us that summer, and after we came home from vacation, we asked if she would like to stay through the year. It was her passion to attend the Capernwray Bible School in Canada, and we were happy to support her in that effort. She lived with us for over two years and became a delight and a blessing to our home. During her time at Bible college, she met Jeremy Reurich, a wonderful young Australian who soon became the love of her life.

On her wedding day as I escorted Jessica to the altar, I was pleased and honored, but I wasn't thinking about all of the blessings of the day. Kathryn and I had devoted a big part of that afternoon to replacing the wedding cake that had fallen apart! It was the true wedding disaster that God solved through a very kindly French lady who rescued us at the very last minute with a new wedding cake. I remember waiting and fretting with Jess as the bridal party's carriage was late, being careful not to hint to the bride about the complications with the cake. As we arrived at the park, I had just one simple, practical thought running through my head as I walked over that uneven ground—"Don't step in a hole! Make sure Jess doesn't trip!" So I wanted to reflect on that wonderful day and gain insight on what God was doing during that high moment in our lives.

People often ask me, "Why pray over our high points? I understand how God heals us when we pray over our low points. But why pray over the best times of our lives? Besides saying "thank you" again, what's to be gained?" Let me give you some things that we have discovered.

Praying Our High Points Tunes Us in to the Activity of God

In our high moments we are often keenly focused on everything that we need to do to make that event a success, such as a wedding, a graduation, or a promotion at work. If we are conscientious, we take careful note of the contributions that key people made for that good thing to happen. We may keep a record and send thank you notes. But as we immerse that wonderful event in reflective prayer, we become increasingly aware of what God was doing to make that event a reality. We gain a glimpse of God's unique and sovereign work. During his ministry, Jesus was fully aware of what his Father was doing. He stayed tuned in through intimate fellowship with his Father. And so he could say:

> Very truly I tell you, the Son can do nothing by himself; he can do only what he sees his Father doing, because whatever the Father does the Son also does.
>
> —John 5:19

Jesus was so attuned to the Father's activity that he could say that the works that he did were not his works at all but were the actions of the Father working through him.

You and I need a training program that helps us tune in to the activity of God in our lives. By meditating and praying about our wonderful moments, we become more aware of what the Father was doing at that time of our lives. Not only that, as we become more aware of God's presence in the past, our hearts become attuned to what he is doing around us in the present and gives us hope for our future.

God Shows Us How He Brought That High Point into Being

As we pray and meditate, not only do we become aware that God was at work, we become aware of *how* he was at work. We become aware of the particular actions God was taking at the time. We increasingly recognize his detailed attention to key turning points along the path; we see how he was arranging events and bringing people together to make this good thing happen.

In chapter 6, we mentioned how God instructed Joshua to place twelve stones at the river's edge to remind future generations of how God stopped the river's flow so the nation could walk across on dry ground. We need our own "stack of stones" reminding us of the good things God has done. It does our hearts good to look back at such events and remember what God did to bring those blessings into our lives.

We See Who God Is in That High Moment of Our Lives

As the children of the generation that crossed the Jordan looked at those stones, they would know what kind of God their parents followed. As they celebrated the Passover, they would look back on their deliverance out of slavery in Egypt, and recognize God as their "Redeemer and Shepherd" (Ex. 15). As they celebrated the Feast of Booths, they would be reminded of how their ancestors lived in tents in the wilderness and how God fought for them and won the victory and became known as "The Lord My Banner" (Ex. 17:15, 16). As they pondered the Ten Commandments, they would look back on the time God had met them at Mount Sinai and given them his law and taken the role of "Our Lawgiver and Judge" (Ex. 20).

When we look back at the high moments of our lives, we see who God was for us then. We learn to thank him for today and to trust him for our future.

By Praying Our High Points, We See That We Owe Everything to God

As we pray over a past moment of triumph or happiness, we realize more and more that we didn't create it through our own strength or ingenuity. Though this great time may have resulted from hard work or careful planning on our part, we realize that the Lord our God had the ultimate hand in bringing it to be. We acknowledge that everything good in our lives comes from him and that our very life's breath is contingent on his divine being. James wrote:

> Every good and perfect gift is from above, coming down from the Father of the heavenly lights, who does not change like shifting shadows.
>
> —James 1:17

Pondering our high points in life helps us honor the Lord and rejoice in him.

Meditation Leads to Genuine Gratitude

Praying and meditating on the good things of our lives leads us to genuine gratitude. We get deeper in touch with the goodness of God. We feel the depth of his kindness in bringing this good thing to be, and our hearts are filled with gratitude. As I prayed over Jessica's wedding day, my heart overflowed with thanks. Like David in Psalm 40:1–3:

> *For the director of music. Of David. A psalm.*
>
> I waited patiently for the LORD;
> he turned to me and heard my cry.
> He lifted me out of the slimy pit,
> out of the mud and mire;
> he set my feet on a rock
> and gave me a firm place to stand.
> He put a new song in my mouth,
> a hymn of praise to our God.
> Many will see and fear
> and put their trust in the LORD.

We Become More Hopeful for the Future

By becoming more thankful for past events, we become more hopeful for the future. We become increasingly confident of God's goodness and look forward to other things he will do as we rely on him. God reassured the generation in exile in Babylon of his future plans of hope for them:

> "For I know the plans I have for you," declares the LORD, "plans to prosper you and not to harm you, plans to give you hope and a future."
>
> —Jer. 29:11

Finally, we should pray over our high points because . . .

It's Good Practice for Praying over Our Low Points.

If we learn how to immerse our high moments in the gracious presence of the Lord, we will know how to immerse our low moments in his care. We'll be able to use the same skill set to pray through the lowest times of our lives, and we will be confident that the same God will meet us and give us what we need.

When you look at your life, you realize that your high points and low points are vitally connected. Think about it—the mountains and valleys of life are made up of the same good earth. The low points of our lives are linked to the high points. It is only one life, not two. The mountain and the valley are features on the same beautiful piece of land. When we become skilled at praying over our high points and discovering how God was at work in those times, we learn that we can use the same skills to pray over our low points. In Psalm 42, one of the sons of Korah details a time of tears and sadness. But then the writer reminds himself of his glorious times of worship when he met with God in the high and holy feast days. He uses the memory of those exalted times to encourage his soul during his days of darkness and shadow:

> *For the director of music. A maskil of the Sons of Korah.*
>
> As the deer pants for streams of water,
> so my soul pants for you, O God.
> My soul thirsts for God, for the living God.
> When can I go and meet with God?
> My tears have been my food

day and night,
while men say to me all day long,
"Where is your God?"
These things I remember
as I pour out my soul:
how I used to go with the multitude,
leading the procession to the house of God,
with shouts of joy and thanksgiving
among the festive throng.
Why are you downcast, O my soul?
Why so disturbed within me?
Put your hope in God,
for I will yet praise him,
my Savior and my God.

—Ps. 42:1–5

Like the psalmist, we need to recall how God has extended his transforming grace into these high moments. Then we'll be careful to look for evidence of his transforming grace in our low moments.

Praying Jessica's Wedding

So it was with great joy that I began to pray over the day I gave Jessica away in marriage. I began by asking, "What did I need most from God at that moment in my life?" As I pondered this, I realized that what I needed was wisdom about how to in some way be a dad to a young bride in her early twenties. What part of God's name related to this need in my life? Well, I did not have to think long to come up with the answer. God is Father! He knows how to be a Father. I could learn a thing or two from him about how to nurture and encourage and love this young woman and her new husband, Jeremy.

So I chose *Father* as my name for God. But then I realized that I needed to be a particular kind of father to Jessica. She was, after all, a fatherless girl. Her birth dad had been absent for all those years. Her stepfathers had trained her to put up with unreasonable demands and harsh conditions in the home. I was going to need God's help in being the kind of dad she needed most. And so I began to think

108

about the kind of Father that God is, the special ways he relates to the many needs of his sons and daughters. I was led to a title that is applied to God in Psalm 68 where he is described as, "a Father to the fatherless." That would be my name for God—Father of the Fatherless. That is what he was for Jessica. He had been faithful to her all through her growing up years. Now he would be faithful to me as I filled this role in her life. So I prayed over Psalm 68:1–6:

For the director of music. Of David. A psalm. A song.

May God arise, may his enemies be scattered;
may his foes flee before him.
As smoke is blown away by the wind,
may you blow them away;
as wax melts before the fire,
may the wicked perish before God.
But may the righteous be glad
and rejoice before God;
may they be happy and joyful.
Sing to God, sing praise to his name,
extol him who rides on the clouds—
his name is the LORD—
and rejoice before him.
A father to the fatherless, a defender of widows,
is God in his holy dwelling.
God sets the lonely in families,
he leads forth the prisoners with singing;
but the rebellious live in a sun-scorched land.

—Ps. 68:1–6

I spent several sessions praying lectio divina over this psalm. First of all, I was reminded that God placed Jessica in our family. More than putting a boarder into our house, more than putting a guest into our spare bedroom, God had placed a daughter into our family. As verse six says, "God sets the lonely in families."

The second thing I noticed was that God was fighting for our family. As I prayed, I recognized that it is a warfare psalm. It is about God scattering his enemies, putting unjust rulers to flight. I saw that

Jessica had grown up in a war zone, and God gave me the insight that he had been fighting for and defending this young woman for a long time. Not only was God the Father of the Fatherless, but he is also the Father who is a warrior. Our God is a warrior God. During her childhood, the hot fire of God's love surrounded Jessica. He brought her to his church. She met Jesus and fell in love with him for a lifetime. She met good men like Pastor Bruce Ingram and saw that there is another way for men to be. God had replaced hurtful people from Jessica's past with peacemakers. God gave her a gentle husband who protects her and defends her as her heavenly Father has done. As God brought Jessica through spiritual conflict, he also took Kathryn and me through a war zone to get to her. Our battle with infertility taught us to yield to God and wait on him for the good gifts that he intends to give.

In my reflections I began to understand that at the time Kathryn and I were going through our adult-sized pain, God was leading Jessica through her childhood pain. When he brought us together, comfort overflowed. As I reflected on the psalm God brought me to a place of rejoicing. I spent several lectio divina sessions with this psalm focused on just that one word—*rejoice!*

> But may the righteous be glad
> and rejoice before God;
> may they be happy and joyful.
>
> —Ps. 68:3

By praying over this high point in my life, I understood more deeply that God has given Kathryn and me a high and holy place in Jessica's life. It is not a creation of my own mind, nor is it a fantasy, a fancy, an invention. No. God had been working on this project for a long time, and he's still working on it. So my breath prayer became, "Father of the Fatherless, Thank you for placing me as Jessica's dad." To this day, it is still a work in progress.

Consider a High Point in Your Life

Let me encourage you to pray over a high point in your life. Consider perhaps the best day you've had . . . ever. Take time to celebrate God's goodness in making that day happen. Recognize the truth of James 1:17:

> Every good and perfect gift is from above, coming down from the Father of the heavenly lights, who does not change like shifting shadows.

Prayerfully consider how God is still at work, maximizing the impact of those wonderful gifts of people and events that contributed to this good thing that took place.

Journal your insights.

Recognize that even in the high moments of our lives, we are in great need of God. Consider the following questions:

What did you need most from God at that time?

What name of God best corresponds to your soul's need of that moment?

What then would be an appropriate breath prayer for your high moment?

Now take a walk and pray your high point breath prayer. When you return, take some time to journal about your prayer.

Now seek out a lectio text for your high point. When you have found it, pray lectio over your text and journal your insights.

Take time again for a walk, praying your high point breath prayer and thinking about your lectio text. When you return from your walk, pray another session of lectio on your selected text and journal your insights.

Keep your breath prayer and lectio text in your devotions for several days. See how the Lord speaks to you.

API Participants Respond

Overall, most people have less to say about high point processing than about how they work through low points. Perhaps that is because we focus so much on problem solving that we fail to notice when it is actually going well with us.

Karen quoted the purpose of peak moment processing: "It awakens us to the presence and purpose of God in the stories of our lives.... He has been with you through the high points, too!"

Charles: "I believe God is leading me in the high point exercise. I acquired a fresh high point, a name of God, and a breath prayer, and I got to share with my brothers!"

In answer to the question, "What was most meaningful today?" Phil wrote: "The high point breath prayer! The restful time of putting together the pieces that made up the highest high point for me—marrying Linda and life with her in grace."

Judith spoke with nostalgia about the heady days of the Jesus Movement. She describes a huge sense of something eternally important going on. At API we ask the seemingly out-of-place question: "What did you need from God during that time?" Maybe sometimes the answer is, "Nothing. I don't need a thing. Or maybe just to say, 'Thank you.'"

In early 2014, Marlee completed a timeline decade by decade. "As I filled in the years, I came to 2004. I recalled that first Saturday in 2004 when God shifted my career focus. I filled in the gaps for this decade and was astounded at all the high points I had experienced. It was truly an enriching experience to pause and reflect on this past decade and observe how God had caused my life to flourish in so many dimensions." She captured the sustaining everlastingness of a spiritual high point in reflection on Kay Arthur's book, *Lord, I Want to Know You.*[46] "The first memory verse I remember my daddy teaching me was Proverbs 18:10, 'The name of the Lord is a strong tower; the righteous run in and they are safe.' I was probably seven or eight.

Every night before bed he would drill me on this verse. Looking back, I realize that dad knew he couldn't always be by my side to protect me, so what he did was plant this promise deep within my spirit so that when I needed protection, I knew to call on the name of the Lord." A high-point experience is a gift that keeps on giving.

Rick: "This was especially new and meaningful to me. I saw in my high point how the Holy Spirit was preparing me for the spiritual battles within that are very serious for genuinely training up new harvest workers in our Portland urban centers."

The next several responses were reflections written during the retreat we call Praying Our Triumphs and Challenges. At this retreat we spend most of a day processing a selected low point on our timelines. Often the turn to a high point is received with relief and joy.

Ken: "Hitting the high point today was the best and most meaningful [part of today's retreat activities]. Jehovah Jireh has always provided more than what I ask or need.

Stan's word of hope for this retreat was hope itself. This hope was fulfilled, "to a great extent" and the anxiety he had was relieved. Hope can be a great high-point gift from God – especially when it springs from a low-point.

Linda agreed that [the most meaningful part of the day's activities] was "getting to focus and write about my high point. Yippee and praise God!"

Gretchen was happy to examine her high point after a day of low-point prayers. She said it was quite meaningful.

CHAPTER 9

THE ART OF SOUL FRIENDSHIP

Carry each other's burdens, and in this way you will fulfill the law of Christ.

—Gal. 6:2

Who do you talk to when your soul needs a friend?

You may have work friends and hobby friends. You may have school friends and old family friends, buddies from way back and new friends you've just met. Who do you talk with when your soul needs a friend?

It's like this: you've prayed, and nothing seems to be happening. Trouble has caught you by surprise and your soul clouds over like a misty day at the ocean. You know God is there, but it's been a good while since you felt his presence, and you are just not sure what is wrong. You listen for his voice, but the signals seem to get crossed, and you wonder if you are simply listening to the imaginations of a barren soul. You bear down and do your spiritual duty, but you know you are gritting your teeth and just getting through. It's clear that your heart is out of shape, and you are not sure what it needs.

If you are fortunate, you may be part of a band of brothers who share life together. You may have a group of sisters who love and laugh and pray and give. Among them there may be that one who

115

has an open heart, a listening ear, and a willingness to pray deeply. Perhaps you have a godly parent or grandparent who listens to your heart. Perhaps you are that person. People come to you. You listen to their stories. You ask questions, you give counsel, you pray, and you hope that your presence makes a difference in their lives. You are experiencing what the ancient Celtic Christians called being a *soul friend*. Whatever you might call this person this is someone who is able to counsel you concerning the health of your soul—and particularly your soul's connection to the living God.

But what kind of person should we seek out to share the sacred things of our soul? What kind of person should we be becoming if we find people seeking us out? What are the qualities that make a good soul friend?

Listening to the Stories of Our Lives

When we set out to pray the stories of our lives, we find that we often need the wisdom of someone who listens well and who can point us to the Lord and his Word. Especially when we are challenged by our low points, we may need the advice and counsel of such a spiritually mature believer.[47] I found such a person in a surprising place for a Baptist pastor—in a Catholic monastery.

Let me tell you about Father Placidus Sander, a good friend to my soul. When I came to know him, he had lived as a Benedictine monk for over sixty years. I met him at Westminster Abbey in Mission, British Columbia, after the death of my father.

My father died on May 4, 2012. I was exhausted by the days of personal care my brothers and our wives gave to Dad during the final weeks of his life. After he passed, I spent a week preparing the graveside and memorial services for this excellent man. I remember looking at the list of things to do early in the week and recalled how much energy it had taken to do the same tasks the year before when our mother had passed away. With the lessons of that grief in mind, I knew that I would need a few days of personal retreat after all was said and done.

Kathryn and I have been taking personal retreats for several years now. When we get to that point when the stresses of life pile up, we know to take two or three days in a very quiet place and disengage from the regular duties of life. We sleep a lot. We read our journals. We have extended devotions. We'll take a half day of silence. Then we'll go for a long walk at noon. And in the afternoon we'll talk about what we gained from our morning with God. We don't watch TV, look at the Internet, text, or make phone calls. We get alone with God and with each other to get refreshed. And sometimes I will go on retreat on my own for a few days.

But I had learned from my mother's death that I needed something more than a personal time away. I wanted to tell my story to a wise elder. I needed someone who could direct my attention to the Lord in a way that would give me a pathway for my grief. I did not want to languish in the valley of the shadow of death. I wanted to walk through it with Jesus. And for that, I needed someone to help me assess how Jesus was with me in this exhausting season of grief. I needed a spiritual director, a soul-friend, a fresh set of eyes for the pathway I was on, someone who knows the ways of the soul.

A pastor friend of mine had told me about a retreat that he had been on at a Catholic monastery in Oregon. My friend serves in the evangelical Christian and Missionary Alliance, and his pastors' group had been to Mount Angel Abbey in Oregon. I had read about monastic tradition while doing research for my doctoral dissertation and learned that the spiritual practices of the monastery had had a tremendous impact on the Protestant revivals dating from the fifteenth century. Martin Luther, the great reformer, was an Augustinian monk and priest teaching at the University of Wittenberg in Germany. After he understood that the gift of salvation came by grace alone through faith alone, he unleashed a spiritual revolution. In the early days of the reformation in Germany, Luther emptied the monasteries. Monks and nuns who had been devoted to prayer within the walls of their cloisters now began to marry and form Christian homes. They brought with them their devotion to daily prayer and Bible reading. These practices became the foundation for evangelical family piety. I grew up in an evangelical Christian home with my parents reading the Bible to us and leading us in family prayer. To this day, in the monastery, the

117

monks and nuns pray and read from the Bible several times each day. They practice what is known as spiritual direction, consultation, or soul-friendship. How is your connection to God? What is it like when you pray? I called Mount Angel and learned that they did not have room for me. Then I called another friend who had told me about Westminster Abbey in Mission, British Columbia. I was glad when they said that there was room, and that there was a good possibility that I could meet with a spiritual director.

I drove up to Canada, nervous, distracted by the details of the directions to the place. I arrived a bit before 3:00 p.m. and went to the guest house where I was greeted by Brother Morris. Born in Holland before World War II, he had been in the monastery for fifty-seven years. He remembers when German paratroopers landed in his homeland in 1940. He was eleven years old. His parents had died when he was just a boy. He told me that in some monasteries, the brothers may go to visit family if there is a need such as sickness or death. Brother Morris showed me to the second floor where my room had a view directly across to the church with its massive bell tower.

Father Mark, the priest in charge of guests, showed me the two dining rooms, one a former chapel where the brothers ate and one downstairs where guests often ate. I would be eating with the monks for some meals—some I would be with other guests. One meal I would be on my own. Father Mark let me know that he had arranged a spiritual direction appointment for me with Father Placidus, who would contact me later.

I went to my room and looked through my journal. I read the graveside service I had written for my mother. As my tears welled up, I felt drawn to pray for the peace of the Holy Spirit. By God's grace, the stress of grief turned to a quiet ease. At 4:00 p.m. I decided to nap instead of taking a walk, and I slept deeply until 5:05. Then I walked across the grounds, trying to clear the cobwebs from my brain before 5:30 prayers in the chapel and dinner afterwards. Later, I wrote of my experience in poetic form:

I walked the grounds, shaking off sleep
To the viewpoint—
Suburbia below the overlook
Then the river,
The farms, the hills,
And Mount Baker,
Viewing the majestic peak from the north,
A new way of seeing the mountain
That dominates the horizon
From my Washington home.

Bells ring,
Calling me to my first vespers.
Brother Morris to his fourth prayers
Of this fifteenth day of May 2012.
His fifty-seventh year
Of daily prayers.
How is your soul, Brother Morris?

The monks
Proclaiming Thy holy Word
Thirty-five black-robed brothers,
Young, old, come in pairs
Bowing before the altar of Jesus.
Those bent with age
Bow less.
Those vigorous
And young
Bow before
A lifetime of submission.
In this moment,
In the next,
Till death.
Life bowed down
Before the Savior.

The cathedral is a great concrete vault,
Statuary engraved
In common cement.
Monks chant.
Echoes of
Imperceptible hallelujahs
Reverberate.
Blue glass for sky
Yellow for sun,
Red for blood
Violet grey light
Streams onto common cement.

Flow in us,
Light of grace
In common earth
Grey stone hearts in need of
Thy light.

The first psalms of vespers,
129, 130, 131.
O Lord, I present to you
A stilled,
A quieted
Soul.

Glory be to the Father
And to the Son
And to the Holy Ghost.
As it was in the beginning
World without end.

A reading from Romans 8:28-29:

And we know that in all things God works for the good of those
who love him, who have been called according to his purpose.
For those God foreknew he also predestined to be conformed to

the image of his Son, that he might be the firstborn among many brothers and sisters.

Shape us, O Lord
In Thy divine image.

Three young men at worship
In plain clothes
One of them must have driven here
In the Boss 1970 red Mustang parked outside.
Now he stands before Jesus
Contemplating his life's journey.
An older couple to my far left
And I
Contemplate where we have been
Coming before Jesus.

After dinner I meet with Father Placidus, an aged yet energetic priest and monk. We met in the sun-drenched conference room. Father Placidus selected chairs and positioned them in the shade offered by the walls between the windows open to the western sun. He specifically arranged my chair with the better view to the garden below with its blooming red azaleas and white dogwoods. I sense that the vivid blossoms of spring are big events for a man who has lived on this hill for over sixty years. He sits opposite me, adjusts his flowing black robe, and asks, "What brings you to black-robed country, Wes?"

I speak of my work as a pastor and teacher, and he exclaims, "You are a long way from home!" I tell him of my grief journey, and he listens intently. He asks me if I see this grief as a gift from God.

He speaks of his own journey of grief, the loss of his brother in recent days. I recall the fresh grave that I had seen in the monks' cemetery while on my walk. He directs me to consider that in death, all of us submit to the monastic vows of poverty, chastity, and obedience. He speaks of the purpose of life to be gift, acceptance, and community. These three things, he says, when all is stripped away, are the things we treasure most.

He spoke of what Jean Vanier discovered in his year of living with the most mentally challenged after he had resigned from his sixteen years as director of L'Arche, a ministry of compassion to the mentally and physically broken. He said he discovered the heart of holiness– what even the most helpless of the people there could be: gift, acceptance, and community. He said that of a woman with Down syndrome and of a man in the extreme weakness of Parkinson's—they were still gift, acceptance, community.

I say that this is what we had experienced with Dad in his closing days.

I told him that Kathryn had said that she felt I was not fully present to her for months after Mom's death. So he spoke of us being present to one another by communion with Jesus, to help one another live in such communion with Jesus so that when he calls us home, we are right there present with him, already prepared to enter his presence.

Then he suggested 2 Corinthians 6:1–2 as the air to breathe, the environment to luxuriate in during the time I was on retreat:

> As God's co-workers we urge you not to receive God's grace in vain. For he says, "In the time of my favor I heard you, and in the day of salvation I helped you." I tell you, now is the time of God's favor, now is the day of salvation.

He notes how in these verses Paul quotes from Isaiah 49:8 but changes the Old Testament text to read, "*Now* is the acceptable time, *now* is the day of salvation!" (emphasis mine). And then the old priest nearly comes up out of his chair as he exclaims with compelling energy, "*Eu-pros*, Wes! *Eu-pros!*" My mind races back to my seminary Greek, and realize he is talking about what favor means: "*Goodness toward you, Wes, the goodness of God coming toward you!*"

Then Father Placidus points out how Paul does a puzzling thing. In this discussion of divine favor, Paul lists the diverse sufferings that befell him:

We put no stumbling block in anyone's path, so that our ministry will not be discredited. Rather, as servants of God we commend ourselves in every way: in great endurance; in troubles, hardships and distresses; in beatings, imprisonments and riots; in hard work, sleepless nights and hunger; in purity, understanding, patience and kindness; in the Holy Spirit and in sincere love; in truthful speech and in the power of God; with weapons of righteousness in the right hand and in the left; through glory and dishonor, bad report and good report; genuine, yet regarded as impostors; known, yet regarded as unknown; dying, and yet we live on; beaten, and yet not killed; sorrowful, yet always rejoicing; poor, yet making many rich; having nothing, and yet possessing everything.

—2 Cor. 6:3–10

But in them all, God's goodness was rushing toward him! "*Eu-pros*, Wes! *Eu-pros!*"

Father Placidus suggested that for today and tomorrow morning, I focus my meditations on 2 Corinthians 6:2, and when I have done that, move on to verses 3–10. And then he added, "Yes, rest, sleep," and he quoted Shakespeare's Macbeth, "Sleep knits the unraveled sleeve of care." Then he speaks of the *now* as the *kairos* moment—that wonderful New Testament concept of time as the critical intersection of opportunity and need. He offers to meet again tomorrow, and I tell him, "I would treasure that." And he rushes off to evening vigils and I to my small room to learn from the silence of my cell.

I meditate upon 2 Corinthians 6. I think about Paul's wonderful word of favor—God's goodness coming at you! He proclaims that even in, or perhaps especially in—all these hardships, God's saving grace is coming at you in all its fullness. My thoughts turn to the deaths of my parents and I begin to write:

As Mom's strength was taken from her
in the ravages of Parkinson's,
   Now is the day of God's favor.
As Dad's strength decayed

in the disaster of pancreatic cancer,
   Now is the day of God's favor.
As we stood at Mom's graveside,
   Now is the day of God's favor.
As we placed flowers upon Dad's lowered casket,
   Now is the day of God's favor.
As we lay sleepless with grief upon our beds,
   Now is the day of God's favor.
As we rise weary, bleary-eyed, and muddled,
   Now is the day of God's favor.

All is:
   Gift.
      Acceptance.
      Communion.

The Gospel opposites of:
   Taking.
      Rejecting.
      Isolation.

The wisdom of Father Placidus helped me first to see the goodness of God in our family sorrow and also to find peace.

The next morning I rose at 4:00 a.m. to view the sunrise from the Eagle's Nest, a prayer room on the top floor of the monastery. I rest in 2 Corinthians 6:2. As the moonlight dances over the flowing Fraser River, the lights of the valley floor flicker on as the world goes about its business. I ponder the *now* of the new life: *In the day of your disaster, I heard you! I helped you!* The day of our disaster became the day of God's favor, the day of salvation. So it was with Dad's days, so it is with this day. The Lord hears. The Lord helps. I am heard. I am helped. I recall the vision God had given Dad in the week before he died. "It's beautiful! It's beautiful!" he exclaimed! "What's beautiful?" I ask.

"The light," he says, "the light!"

I heard you. I helped you.

At 8:45 a.m. I go to the bench at the overlook and sit in sunshine gazing out over the Fraser River and the valley below. I decide to be still and quiet with one word for thirty minutes. *Favor.* I have stilled and quieted my soul: *Favor. Favor.*

God's intent: *favor.*

My consent: *Receive the favor of the Lord.*

After thirty minutes, I snooze in the sunshine upon God's bench, the gentle breeze cooling the skin of my neck.

I met with Father Placidus later in the day and tell him about my thirty minutes of silence on the bench. He muses about how the Greek of Ephesians 1:12 speaks of how wonderful it is simply to exist in God's presence, "in order that we, who were the first to put our hope in Christ, might *be* to the praise of his glory" (emphasis mine).

Once again I am struck with his passion for Scripture and especially for his love of the Greek text of the New Testament. He has meditated deeply on these texts. And I appreciate how he relates the events of my life to the wonderful words of life given once for all to the saints. Just be. Not do. Not perform. Just be. As the day comes to a close, I am surprised at the level of ease in my soul. The grief has waned. It is still present but the exhaustion has eased.

What lessons emerge?

What made Father Placidus a fruitful soul friend, a helpful spiritual director for me?

1. He listened to my story and connected it to God's story. This is the foremost necessity—listening to God as you listen to the story of your friend. You are looking for what God is doing in the life of your friend.

2. Then he asked me if I see this grief as a gift from God. He wanted me to see that God was actively involved in my story. Jeannette Bakke has written that "stories of spiritual direction are stories of God embodied in the particularity of individual lives."[48] As Father Placidus listened to my story he also was listening for the story of God.

3. He referred me to a particular place in the script of God's story, and I found solace in those verses of Scripture.

4. He related his life story to mine, but then returned to my life story. He invited me to consider that he, too, was an experienced traveler on the pathway of grief. The evidence of the fresh grave in the cemetery let me know that I had a friend who understood. Much later I was to learn that his two brothers had passed on to the Lord during the days of my own grief.

5. He encouraged me to meditate on the connection between my reality and the reality of Scripture. His passion for Scripture connected my grief to the concrete experience of the Apostle Paul. Through my meditations I saw and felt the comfort of the Gospel. Through 2 Corinthians 6, God's healing grace was poured out upon me in the face of suffering. He recommended a singular Scripture for my meditation. I spent two days meditating on that single text. I prayed over it. I wrote about it in my journal. I connected that passage with my story. I sat in the sunshine with a single word from that passage. I was surprised at how strong I felt after those two days; how much of the burden of grief had been lifted.

6. He respected my capacity to hear God through Scripture. He did not attempt to teach me what God wanted me to hear. He explained to me the meaning of the passage, and trusted the Holy Spirit to guide my soul.

7. He affirmed what I had experienced, and connected that to Scripture. He listened to my story of being still for those thirty minutes on the bench, meditating on the word *favor*. And then he affirmed through a single word in Ephesians 1:12 that just being with God brings glory to him.

8. He indicated his willingness to meet with me again. And for that I was very grateful.

What did I do that made my time with Father Placidus especially useful to my journey?

1. I told him what I needed.
2. I listened to what he had to say.
3. I wrote extensive notes of my time with him and my times with God.

4. I immersed myself in the Scriptures he recommended.
5. I rested!
6. I reflected.
7. I went back and saw him again.

Jeannette Bakke has wisely written about the responsibilities of each person in the spiritual direction relationship:

> Directors and directees are dedicated to listening for God's ways, desires and invitations. They meet together to listen to the Holy Spirit and to each other, for the benefit of the directee. Ultimately, though, the conversations are for God, because as directees become more attuned to God, their life and actions will reflect more of God's desires. Opening our ideas and feelings with another person and intentionally inviting God to be present is like "opening the windows of a closed house to spring air."[49]

Spirit-centered listening requires an intimate knowledge of the ways of God on the part of the one listening and willingness on the part of the one speaking to be open to the voice of God. Anderson and Reese, in their excellent book, *Spiritual Mentoring*, point to the opportunity we have to gain a deeper understanding of God's activity in the story of our life. They speak of the tragedy of the unexamined life: "Entire lives are lived without recognizing the plot that God has woven into the days and nights of time."[50] Discerning God's plot in the story of our lives is one of the great benefits of ongoing spiritual mentoring. In soul friendship, we are seeking someone who can listen for the echoes of God's voice in the plotline of our life story. As Anderson and Reese put it, "A good mentor will help us 'read between the lines' for the hidden and earthy messages that God will give because life is full of God."[51] Good mentors will walk the journey with us, and show us how our story connects to the great story of Christ: "As companions on the journey, mentors intentionally and carefully help others listen to their lives, ask their own questions, connect their story to The Story, the Jesus Story."[52]

API Participants Respond

In November, Dave wrote about a soul friendship triads exercise: "This was very meaningful—we as men were able to share; the men listened to me and prayed for me—discussed what their breath prayers had meant to them. Good encounter with God." In April he wrote, "My soul friend partner and I are gaining trust." By May, Dave reported that he had formed a soul friend relationship and had been practicing listening while praying very often.

In October Ken wrote, "A meaningful time together with two guys who love the Lord." In November he observed, "Flexibility was key here. One was struggling while the other two listened and prayed. We affirmed the breath prayer of the one struggling." By May, he wrote of intimacy: "I enjoyed my time with [my soul friend partner] and had the opportunity to pray with and for him. The level of intimacy is something guys do not share often."

After the first retreat Phil said of the soul friendship triads: "The interactions brought us to more intimate fellowship (spiritual, not intellectual—*real*)." At the second retreat he wrote: "I love the Walk 'N Talks and the men's sharing and prayer. My partner in this exercise is a joyful and deep brother. I greatly enjoyed time with him." Later he shared this from his journal: "Gentle, manly fellowship and prayer time, quietly connecting."

At the February seminar we practiced prayerful listening as we shared about our timeline breath prayer. From Gretchen's evaluation: "I loved my partner's honesty, loved praying while listening— it shuts off my non-helpful mind chatter." At the second retreat, Praying Our Triumphs and Challenges, Gretchen said, "I'd say the soul friendship session was the pivotal point of the retreat. I felt supported and understood. . . . I have realized that [God's presence in the] spirit of the other person... is the foundation for the soul friendship conversation."

In February we introduced the idea of stealth soul friendship in which we prayerfully listen unbeknownst to the one talking. Judith wrote: "I loved this particular assignment—its potential ongoing usefulness. I've been using this in classes at school. It works—light comes into the world and the darkness cannot overcome it."

At the October retreat, Stan characterized the value of soul friendship triads as, "Essential, Irreplaceable." And the soul friendship walk as the most meaningful part of the retreat. A few weeks later at the November seminar, he wrote that, "[The soul friendship triad exercise was] the part I dread most but need most. Certainly it bears fruit for me but this one doesn't come easily to such communal intimacy." In February he reported about working in soul friend pairs. "Always good for me to pull back into the needs of someone besides myself." And finally, in May Stan wrote that, "[soul friendship processing] was a helpful time of reflection from a partner who really resonates with me."

At the first seminar, Robin struggled a little: "It was new to me so I wasn't really catching on to the flow at first, but I'm looking forward to exploring this further." In November she reported, "This was an awesome time of sharing. It is getting easier as we practice." At the February retreat: "[The soul friendship session was] wonderful! Great questions that led me deeper. . . . It helped me see things I wouldn't have seen on my own" And, "API has encouraged me over the past year to pray and listen to the Holy Spirit when I am with others. It really helped me as I spent time this past year with a friend who was in the last stages of life. Learning the art of soul friendship helped me know what to say, what Scriptures to share, what songs to sing, what to pray, and how to share hope in a difficult situation."

At the Art of Soul Friendship retreat Marlee wrote: "I loved sharing with my soul friend—it was so cleansing. Like me, she is a bit of a maverick, so we were well paired. I loved her listening ear." At the January seminar she reported, "I loved being the pray-er [in a triad]. It taught me more about loving the speaker for the glory of God revealed in her. How might that prayer pull excellence out of her?" During the March seminar Marlee and Judith were paired to practice soul friendship. Marlee wrote: "So good. Judith made one statement after I had muddled around awhile, and it was like the Lord himself was speaking to me with razor sharp insight that will keep me listening and processing for some time."

In January, Linda wrote: "This is really constructive, effective!" At the March seminar she wrote: "I had unexpected help and sweet time with my soul friend! I wasn't looking for much and got tons (smiley face)!" At the Art of Soul Friendship retreat, she observed that reviewing the biblical and historical perspective on soul friendship and spiritual direction, "reassures me that we're not out on some new-age limb, that, in fact, the roots are quite old but have been lost." On the end-of-year evaluation, Linda remarked that she didn't practice praying while listening nearly enough, but that it was good to know how!

At the February seminar, Charles was enthusiastic about the soul friendship experience. "It was just plain good to share with two brothers! All manner of supportive and encouraging engagements are around me and even including me. The word *love* comes to mind." At the Art of Soul Friendship retreat, he wrote of the assigned pairs: "Pull up a chair and listen for an hour or two." Of group discussions he wrote: "Immensely important (if it's true that we are members of *one* body—and it *is* true.)" Charles indicated that he hoped to participate in soul friendship at every opportunity and also that he has already been doing something very close with other people.

In December, Rick gave the soul friendship sessions five stars which he drew in with exclamations marks. He wrote, "Hearing Wes and Dave share and pray really helped me begin to grasp signature Scripture." Rick gave the soul friendship pairs exercise at the March seminar the top score. He added that it was, "Most excellent—releasing and freeing!" In April he wrote that he, "especially loved sharing deeply" with the two men in his triad.

Being taught early in life not to pry, Karen sometimes felt intrusive when asking questions aimed at seeking out God's hand in a story. However, she loved the idea of *stealth* soul friendship that just allowed her to listen and pray. A year later, she said of the soul friendship experience at a seminar, "Really developing this year. I look forward to more times of soul friendship. It is a time to really get to know the heart and soul of your friend. What a sweet time! Bring it on!" At the Praying Our Triumphs and Challenges retreat, Karen was paired with Gretchen to process low points. She said: "I loved walking with Gretchen and being able to share together the things we are grieving."

Questions to Ponder
1. What are your hopes for beginning or strengthening your journey of soul friendship? What one word best expresses that hope?
2. What fears may be stirring in you as you consider telling your story to a soul friend? What one word best expresses your fear?
3. Of the characteristics of a soul friend that Father Placidus demonstrated, which are most attractive for you?
4. Of the characteristics that I (Wes) demonstrated in receiving soul friendship, which are most essential for you at this time?

Steps to Engage
1. Consider these words of Jeannette Bakke and recall the people in your life who have been a soul friend to you:

"There are probably many persons who have acted as spiritual directors but have not used that term in describing themselves. C. S. Lewis is an example of such a person. His teaching, books, and letters were filled with an attentiveness to the Holy Spirit rather than generalized advice giving."[53]

2. Take time now to list the people in your life who have been particularly attentive to the Holy Spirit and who have listened well to you.

3. As you consider your need for a soul friend or spiritual director, consider how God has directed you through the fellowship of his church. Consider this statement from Henri Nouwen, and make a decision to listen more fully to the voice of the Holy Spirit in the life of your church: "The church itself is a spiritual director: it tries to connect your story with God's story. Just to be part of this community means you are being directed, you are being guided, you are being asked to make connection."[54] As you listen to your friend at the next coffee break at church, recognize that you may be treading upon holy ground. Listening in this manner is like making a prayer without words.

4. Take time now to create a breath prayer expressing your word of hope for finding a soul friend or perhaps renewing a soul friendship.

5. Take time as well to create a breath prayer addressing your word of fear.

6. Conclude your reflections in a time of prayer. Bring your thoughts and longings to the Friend beyond all friends, the Wonderful Counselor who leads you into all truth.

CHAPTER 10

PRAYING IN COMMUNITY

Therefore if you have any encouragement from being united with
Christ, if any comfort from his love, if any common sharing in
the Spirit, if any tenderness and compassion, then make my joy
complete by being like-minded, having the same love, being one
in spirit and of one mind. Do nothing out of selfish ambition or
vain conceit. Rather, in humility value others above yourselves,
not looking to your own interests but each of you to the interests
of the others.

—Phil. 2:1–4

Let's go back to where we started: back to the retreat center with
its towering cedar trees, flowing pools, and seeking hearts.
Think back to that first chapter, and remind yourself of the word
of hope that you selected. What were you hoping to receive as you
read this book? Let me ask . . . to what degree have you received it?

As you have read this book, it is my hope that you have learned
skills of personal meditation on Scripture, plunged into the heart
of God through breath prayer, pondered the low points and high
points of your life, and prayerfully reflected on how God has been
at work shaping you throughout your lifetime. This is the core of
the Awakenings retreat experience.

But there is one important element that is missing. We have found that this part of the Awakenings experience is essential and transformational. What is it?

The other people in the room.

Yes, we've shared some of their stories throughout this book. But there's nothing like listening, learning, speaking, and sharing in person.

On retreat, there are several different roles played out by the people in the group.

First: the teacher. On retreat, our teaching team introduces the prayer skills and gives biblical and historical backgrounds to each one. We share books, stories, and personal examples of how these prayer skills work out. I have sought to fulfill this role in the pages of this book.

Second: the coach. As you have read the book, you have learned, and I hope, tried out new approaches to prayer. What was it like when you went on your first breath prayer walk? Did you wonder if you were doing it right? In seminars and on retreat, you can meet with a seasoned coach who will give you feedback on your experience in real time. On that first breath prayer walk, you may stop by and whisper your emerging breath prayer to a coach who may ask you a clarifying question, offer a word of counsel, or simply speed you on your way.

Third: your fellow seekers. The table discussions on retreat can be amazing. For example, after we finish a lectio session, the leader will typically ask, "What was it like to be silent with this passage?" People will share their experience of trying to get quiet, of seeking to still their minds, of trying to focus on the Scripture while the noises in the room drew their attention away. You discover that other people share your struggles. Then the leader will ask, "What did you gain from your reflections on the passage?" This becomes a rich time of relating truth that we have experienced from God. You will discover that others will bring new thoughts in addition to the insights and blessings you received in your lectio time.

Here is what some participants have said about the value of hearing from the other people in the room:

"Very valuable—my learning is multiplied by diverse input." – Linda, 2014.

"Immeasurable! Meat! Couldn't replace this time." – Monica, 2014.

"The group is very open and safe with each other." – Phil, 2014.

"Eye opening and shedding a different light/perspective. The trust we have for each other is powerful." – Kay, 2014.

"Good because they force me to process the information and communicate back to the group." – Ian, 2014.

"So insightful to hear from everyone—nuggets of gold are generously shared." – Marlee, 2014.

Finally, you gain a soul friend or two. During the retreat you take several walks alone, praying your breath prayer, journaling, or pondering your personal timeline or lectio passage. When you return, we ask each person to join a small group and talk about how the time went. We like to do this in threes, with one person serving as the listener, one person telling their story, and one person silently praying. Each person has about fifteen minutes to tell what their experience has been like, and then you rotate roles. As you participate in a soul friendship triad, you discover how surprising it can be to have the full attention of two people who are on the journey with you. Learning to listen like that and be heard in this way brings a quiet confidence and peace.

Here are some comments from participants about practicing soul friendship:

"[I learned that a] a soul friend is someone who will be able to listen and not try to fix the problem but to ask questions that will direct the person to think about what they need from God." – Kathy, 2014.

"I learned that I don't have to talk all the time." – Sandi, 2014.

"I heard words of love from God about taking better care of myself." – Wes, 2014.

"I learned how to listen to someone in need as I was quiet before the Lord." – Monica, 2014.

"Wow! Each time we do this I feel my faith and prayer become stronger and better defined." – Kay 2014

"This was the best part! It was fruitful and I think the more times I do this the more comfortable I would be with this." – Ian, 2014.

"God gave me a gift last year of being able to be with a friend while he was dying. It was a gift to be able to listen to the Holy Spirit and pray Scripture with him and be able to comfort him. It was the first experience I've had with really being led by the Holy Spirit as I was a soul friend to someone. Usually I've been giving advice to people and trying to help fix their problems." – Robin, 2014.

"[Frank Laubach says in the book we read, *Letters from a Modern Mystic*], 'I hunger, O how I hunger for others to tell me their soul adventures.' This ties in so well with what we are learning in soul friendship!" – Robin, 2015.

Consider the depth of the soul friendship experience recorded in the journal of Dr. Mary Hoppa, a 2013 Soul Friendship Retreat participant:

April 19, 2013 Notes from Soul Friend Session: As a soul friend I wonder if I am asking the right questions. Keep Satan from us. This is near my life . . . my wounds. I feel your comfort. You comfort us so we can comfort others. A wound still scabbed over, not fully healed . . . a knowing of you. A wounded heart, has there been forgiveness? Acceptance? No proving! Your love is like a fountain . . . being or doing . . . in both you love us. We do not have to do anything but if we do your will you are pleased. Do we need to prove to anyone . . . is that futile? To oneself? Is that necessary? To God not needed, Daughter of the Most High God—God's love is our all in all. The next step may be hard but this one is accomplished. The door is open even if only half way. April 20, 2013: I look unto the hills from where my help comes from—my help comes from the Lord! (Ps. 121:1–2) Sharing with my soul friend, Judith, I had something to talk about but I forgot . . . I could not remember. It had seemed so important. So I pick Aaron to talk about. I give a bit of history . . . we process . . . Judith prays . . . She feels immense sorrow. Mine? Ed's? Aaron's? God's? All? She sees a wave, tsunami like, and I begin to see Jesus, as in a scene from Moses, opening up the sea . . . which is before us . . . I am running through, beckoning the others frantically to hurry, hurry! Before the waters close in!

Jesus comes before me in the path and says, "Mary, slow down! I will hold these waters apart for as long as you need . . . do not be afraid to walk through, and do not be afraid that the others will not make it through . . . Judith shares her experience with her daughter. She helps me see Aaron in my mind. I see him fall, she encourages me to cup him in my hands, think how much I love him and then think how much more God loves him. Speak to him in love—even while holding boundaries. Do not go into the darkness with him. Judith reminds me that we, who walk with Jesus, must stay in the light and not cross the line into the darkness. We can beckon Aaron and others to come to us, we do not have to step into the "miry pit." We are not despaired.

I went back to my room and meditated on the story of Moses. All of God's people, the Israelites, made it through the Red Sea. Moses did not fear they would be lost. I see Jesus and me sitting on a bluff overlooking the Red Sea. I say, "I guess you can close it now."

Jesus looks at me and says, "No, not yet . . . you are not comfortable with that."

"But everyone is through," I say.

"But you are not," Jesus replied.

"Ahh, I say," I keep my eyes on Him, "Now I am ready."

"Yes," He says, "Now you are."

—Dr. Mary Hoppa, 2013.

As we see from the experiences of participants on retreat and in the seminars, we gain the wisdom and insights of others on the journey. Here are some other things we have learned as we have studied, listened, and prayed together.

Contemplative Prayer Renews Intercessory Prayer

We have discovered that praying in a contemplative manner can bring new vitality to our times of intercession and corporate prayer.

There was a period of about ten years that I attended an annual pastors' prayer summit which brought together sixty to one hundred pastors from a plethora of churches. Imagine a large meeting room overlooking the ocean, and there being no agenda but to sing, pray, read Scripture, and seek the Lord for the needs in the room and for the cities where the pastors serve. Imagine this going on for four days. Imagine repeating this once each year for ten years. Those were times of great cleansing for me. God killed my denominational prejudice. God deepened my heart with him. He unified the brothers. He renewed passion and launched new vision. Toward the end of those ten years, however, my soul longed to be still and quiet with God. Contemplative prayer became for me that place of intimate contact with God away from the company of others. But then after several years, I went back to a pastors' prayer summit. I engaged the old environment with a new heart. God spoke to me about new goals and dreams. It was wonderful. Contemplative practice had renewed my ability to connect with God in a large group. The lesson emerged: Contemplative prayer renews corporate intercession.

But we have also found that contemplative prayer renews our passion and desire for personal intercessory prayer.

Over the last few years, I have had the privilege of teaching a class on reflective prayer at Bakke Graduate University. One of my students had prayed continually for her alcoholic father, but after many years, had lost heart. On retreat, she became aware that even while directing a national prayer movement, she had given up on praying for her father. That week, contemplative practice renewed her intercessory heart for her dad. Not long after the retreat, God gave her a hint that he was working in her father's life. Through biblical contemplation, her personal intercession for her father gained new hope.

Using Reflective Prayer in Intercessory Prayer Meetings

We have also learned that contemplative practices such as lectio renews the energy of our prayer groups.

Sometimes when we are in a prayer meeting, prayer becomes more about the requests than about God. Rather than assisting our connection with the Lord, the members of the group seem instead to get in one another's way. Perhaps the weight of the prayer requests themselves can challenge the most faithful heart. Or the particular prayer style of a person in the group calls attention to the one praying rather than to the Lord. Integrating a few moments of contemplative practice can draw attention back to God and to his Word and give fresh power to the prayer group. We have also learned that putting a short contemplative prayer time into a longer intercessory prayer meeting refreshes and renews us for continued intercession.

Let me talk about some ways to further integrate contemplative prayer practices into daily life.

Utilizing Breath Prayer

Use triggers to remind yourself to pray your breath prayer. For example, a businessman made the decision that he would pray his Yahweh Shalom breath prayer when he opened the door to his office. A school bus driver prayed his breath prayer for his fellow drivers every time he entered the staff break room. A busy husband and father found quality breath prayer time when he was out walking his dog. You get the idea.

Here is a way to deepen the meaning and purpose of your ministry team. Develop breath prayers for ministry teams. For instance, I began a breath prayer from Luke 10, "Lord of the Harvest, send me to those who would welcome you." After several months of praying this prayer, it became an "us" prayer, and I gave it to our church family: "Lord of the Harvest, send us to those who would welcome you."

You can begin by asking what you need most in relation to the mission of your team. We developed breath prayers for our food bank, worship ministry and other ministries. Here are a few examples with companion Scripture texts for doing lectio:

From the food bank: Lord who fed the multitudes, multiply these small loaves and fishes to glorify your name and bring the lost to you (Mark 16:40–42).

From the worship team: Lord, as we seek your face, unveil our hearts to see your glory (2 Cor. 3:13–18).

From the church council: Lord of the wind and the waves, make us bold in your name (Matt. 14:28–29).

From the trustees: Master builder, enable us to take care of your house so your people can worship and serve in an environment that honors you (Matt. 7:24–27).

From the women's ministry team: Abba Father, your adopted daughters pray that we would grow strong in love and service this year (Phil. 2:4).

Modifying Lectio

Lectio divina can take many forms besides the twenty-five- to thirty-minute format we have introduced. Modify your lectio time to suit your needs. Rather than setting aside twenty-five to thirty minutes, devote just three or four minutes to prayerfully read a passage and then engage in intercession based upon it. In a shortened lectio format, repeat key words and phrases aloud, and let the text soak into your spirit as you read. Take five minutes just now to practice, using the passage from Isaiah 50. Read it over and over for three minutes, and then offer a two minute intercession based upon it. See how it feels.

> The Sovereign LORD has given me an instructed tongue,
> to know the word that sustains the weary.
> He wakens me morning by morning,
> wakens my ear to listen like one being taught.
> The Sovereign LORD has opened my ears, and I have not been rebellious;
> I have not drawn back.
>
> —Isa. 50:4-5

This is how we often begin our prayer and staff meetings at Bethel Church. We then proceed into intercession. You can also use this kind of prayerful reading of Scripture to begin committee and board meetings, thus focusing participants' attention onto the character of God. You can conclude your short prayer by asking God to oversee your group meeting.

Incorporating Silence and Prayer into Ministry Team Meetings

To increase prayer in your ministry team meetings, bring a five-minute hourglass to the table. The first person takes the hourglass and prays silently until the sand runs through. That person then passes it on to the next person. The praying person engages in the discipline of disengagement, speaking to no one but the Lord and bringing the concerns of the current discussion to the Lord. This silently communicates that each person's input, while important, is not always essential to the mission of the team. Rather, it redirects attention to the one Lord who is essential.

Telling Others about Your Contemplative Experience

Create a fifteen- to thirty-second speech describing your contemplative prayer experience. When people ask you how this book has impacted your life, you can tell them in a concise summary. Then consider what you might say if they ask a follow up question.

How You Hope to Integrate the Prayer Skills into Daily Life

Now take five minutes to write a paragraph that expresses your goals and intentions for using the prayer skills in your day-to-day life and ministry.

Finally, consider including the Awakenings prayer guide, *Morning Noon, and Night, a Trinitarian Devotional* in your daily practice. This resource features breath prayer and lectio for daily reflection, as well as a structured time to integrate your own Bible reading and prayers of intercession. The prayer guide is available at our website.

To contact the author, order materials, or find out about the next retreat or seminar, go to www.AwakeningsPrayer.com.

API Participants Respond to Praying in Community

Judith: "I love the sharing and connection. Can't beat it! I respond to all the wisdom sitting in this room." Judith found value whenever the group was given the gist of a revealed heart. In community she also found an aid to discipline. "I need the discipline the group setting brings." And there was something about working in small groups that fulfilled a need that on one retreat she described as, "activating solidarity." Speaking of working in triads, she said, "Love this. It resonates deeply with my extreme need of community." In fact, she wished for more frequent meetings together. "I feel like I would like a half-way meeting—I would like to host something at the two-week mark. I understand that yet another meeting is not necessarily desirable, but something is stirring in my heart."

Marlee: "There is such a sweet spirit and expression of grace in this community. . . . I am revived, more optimistic, and encouraged by the energy and insight of this group." Like Judith, Marlee also appreciated the discipline provided by community. "I so needed today," she wrote in January of 2014. "After a hectic December, I welcomed the discipline of coming together and reducing my focus to one word." About the group discussions she said, "I just love the fellowship around insight on prayer. . . . Love it that they are so authentic—no religion here!"

Stan: "Prudent yet open revelations of self build stronger community." Naturally a loner, Stan grew from connecting with other people during the discussions and soul friendship exercises. About group sharing he writes, "[The large group discussions] return me to a sense of 'normalcy' after hearing the experiences of others . . . these brief glimpses into how others are experiencing the same material helps widen my perspective." But Stan reserved his highest praise for the value of the soul friendship connection: "Corporate prayer is the hardest thing in the world for me. I'm in awe of those who pray freely but am tongue tied myself. The one-on-one counsel [of soul friendship] is critical in refining and focusing the meditation."

Stan grew in his comfort with both group and one-on-one sharing of prayers. About an annual group prayer gathering on a local beach Stan said, "Can we do this once a month?"

Dave: "All of us were really with each other and we made some good connections." On every feedback form, Dave mentioned how much he was really enjoying the fellowship of the group and always appreciated the large group discussions. In November, he observed: "People were very open about what was meaningful to them." In December he used an exclamation point: "I am connected with these guys!" In January he said, "This was good! Nice way of having us connect with one another." And in March: "I am building on a meaningful discussion with Ken; it's nice to have someone I can trust and pray with." And finally, at year's end: "Thoughtful reflections [were shared]. It was nice listening to people's stories—everyone has really benefited and some meaningful, wonderful friendships have begun."

Robin: "It is always so insightful to hear others' spiritual experiences." Concerning group discussions Robin said, "[I am] learning that it is a work in progress all the time . . . I am finding that I love to talk about the deep things of God and all that I am learning." Reflecting on the past: "Much of the praying in community I have experienced are in Moms in Touch groups when my kids were in school. I thought it should be a model of community prayer." And then she looked ahead: "I see many of the things I learned at Moms in Touch at API, and this helps me start thinking about how it can be used in the church."

Gretchen valued community. "Community support" is what she was looking for at the second retreat. One reason she appreciated the group interaction was, "the nature of the people here who shared deeply . . . [it was] honest—we know each other. . . . I love hearing what others say and that this is powerful for them also."

Charles: "Fellowship is always wonderful among believers. . . . I enjoy and am fed by the sharing of others. . . . Sharing/fellowship—what's not to like? . . . Christian fellowship nourishes my life—I'm often starved for such." For Charles, his experience of community went quickly, in his words, "from intimidation to exhilaration" as he enjoyed, "a complete and certain trust" that was established during one-on-one engagement.

Phil: "The group was alive and real. People shared from the heart; we cared for each other." That was written at the first retreat. Keep in mind that Phil is a counselor—he's pretty much all about safe sharing. He elaborated: "The interactions brought us to more intimate fellowship; spiritual, not intellectual, but real. And yes, guys CAN be intimate! But going from the intimacy of a triad to the larger group was difficult for me." At the end of the second year, Phil wrote, "The group was very open and safe with each other."

Linda: "It's just good to share sweetness and discovery with others of like mind." She characterized the value of group discussions as "God arranged," and appreciated the diversity in the group as an aid to learning. Linda was able to connect fairly quickly with others through the nametag exercise described earlier: "It opens people up in surprising and wonderful ways. I get to know them! . . . It reveals personal stuff; helps me feel closer to people—relationships!"

Karen: "I like to hear how God was speaking to each one of us during the month." That was one of four similar comments Karen made about the nametag exercises; like others, she really responded to this icebreaker. "This time helped me get to know others in our group and hear their hopes . . . the start of getting to really know each other." Karen's gentleness and other-focus was a great model for community-building and one of the factors behind why the group came together so quickly.

Ken: "I enjoyed the sharing. It built bonds of friendship." Ken admits that he shies away from sharing much in a group setting, but gained a great deal from listening. He says of the group discussions: "I always enjoy listening to how God is working in people's lives." While appreciating the group bonding, he responded more enthusiastically to intimate times of one-on-one with the other guys.

Rick: "The group sharing was very real soul sharing and meaningful." The words he used most to describe his experience of the group discussion were: excellent, meaningful, and insightful. At the April seminar he elaborated on what made the group click for him: "I always love the genuine honesty—even when one person says, 'I pass' and another guy has to stop talking because he is so overwhelmed with tears."

PARTICIPANTS: WHERE ARE THEY NOW?

We hope that tracking with the participants through their API experience has enhanced your own connection with the Lord. These final reflections will give you a sense of what our participants have gained throughout the year. May your journey be enhanced as you consider what they have gained.

At the end of the 2014 API year, Judith wrote: "Congruent with my growth of silent discipline has been a rekindling of a very deep creative fire. I am wondering—is it just me, or is this common enough that we should address it during the third year? A retreat. An offshoot? . . . I can't stand that [the seminars are] only once a month. It drives me crazy." Later that year, Judith went to Greece for an extended residential poet's workshop. Upon her return, she joined a writer's group. A gifted artist, she staffed a National Day of Prayer event on downtown streets where her live drawings representing prayer for the city encouraged others to express their prayers in art. She is working on ideas for a retreat or workshop that combines the elements of contemplative prayer with creative expression for visual and literary artists—in her words: "creative releases that nurture the spirit."

Marlee writes of a restlessness she was struggling to understand. "I am at that stage of life where I am shrugging duties and focusing on what fills my heart with joy and will leave a legacy for others. I do not embrace duties that God does not call me to embrace. I will not cherish another duty. What I do lust after is more of the spacious place of God's amazing grace from Psalm 18:19, 'He brought me out into a spacious place.' I know it is the place where God delighted in me. I am so very curious about this spacious place; I know it is the place where God speaks and I still myself to listen. . . . My experience with contemplation is elementary, but when I squeeze into that spacious place, it is a place of glory, of revelation, and of mystery. I am never the same. It transforms me; it arrests me; it wrecks me for the ordinary." One of the first breath prayers Marlee shared was, "Bright Morning Star, release your beauty through me." A gifted photographer, Marlee uses her camera almost daily to release the beauty she finds in that spacious place. She traveled to Ireland in the summer of 2015, feeling called to pray and seek healing for a wounded land. You can find her photography at MarleeHuber.com and at facebook.com/MarleeHuber.

Stan connects with God's eternal nature through his history with Israel. He is studying the Hebrew language and enjoys regular fellowship with an assembly of Messianic Jews. Fulfilling a long-standing dream to visit in the land of God's chosen people, he spent four weeks in Israel during the fall of 2015, volunteering with the Israel Defense Force. His first few days in-country were spent in Jerusalem, where he witnessed the chaos and desperation of a region torn by frequent violence. His volunteer assignment in Galilee was no respite from the unrest. Advised to stay clear of Nazareth, he wrote to friends, "[I'm] frustrated by the daily changes to my weekend plans but that's the reality of life in Eratz Yisrael." Just before leaving for Israel, Stan began looking ahead. "I don't know where this is going to lead me. I have been so focused on this trip, I haven't even thought about what comes next." He spoke hopefully of being able to return to Israel with his brother and with his sons when they are old enough to be accepted into the program.

Dave and his wife, Robin, are striving to combine integrity as Christians with authenticity as musicians and leaders in a world often hostile to their faith. In the summer following their first year with API, Dave and Robin conducted their third annual jazz band camp and in September, took one of the groups to the Monterrey Jazz Festival in California.

Robin writes about her experience in API: "Over the last year, I have come out of a long season of being a Martha. I have stepped back from ministry for a while in order to sit at Jesus' feet like Mary did. API came at a time when I was feeling every empty and burned out from doing too much and too many things that were not appointed for me. As I have stepped back from being over-committed, God has allowed me to minister in surprising ways that I never could have conceived of on my own. As I am learning to listen, I am finding peace for the first time. God doesn't need to answer prayers the way I ask in order for me to be OK. I can be at rest in him however he answers because I have him. He is much more than just a fixer of our problems. . . . His loving presence is enough."

Gretchen wrote about her experience of contemplation: "We meditate on earthly things all the time. It follows that we can meditate on God. Contemplation transforms us into loving people. By focusing on the nature of Christ, we become more like Christ . . . I felt great peace, trust, and freedom because I learned ways to just plain focus on God. Wanting to know God brought me to moments of wonderful calmness. I was able to learn more about letting go of myself and enjoying that way of being with God." About midway through her time with API, Gretchen initiated the process of starting and facilitating a seminar series for NAMI, the National Alliance on Mental Illness, where she carried her deep compassion for the suffering of others into their world. She continues to look for ways to live out God's love for all people particularly for those who are marginalized.

Charles lives a life of quiet retirement, spending a great deal of time in the local senior center where he schools many an opponent on the finer points of pool. He enjoys the simple camaraderie there but does not often find fertile ground for sharing insights gained from his contemplative life with the Lord—although he has tried! His ability to listen well and the wisdom that comes from his times of close connection with God make Charles a welcome participant in Christian men's groups.

Phil uses his tremendous gifts of encouragement in a full-time counseling ministry where he not only engages the broken one-on-one, but provides leadership as clinical director of the counseling center. He sees his roles as husband, friend, counselor, pastor, and boss in the light of serving the sovereign Lord. He has incorporated much of what he learned at API into his counseling practice.

Linda's openness comes across with the power of a need: "I've wanted to serve someone and be vulnerable with someone. It's so freeing." Hear her servant's heart in this declaration: "I was so blessed to pray for others and be used of him!" It is not surprising that Linda is deeply committed to her work as a volunteer in a Christian agency that helps women navigate the life-changing and intimate details of pregnancy.

Karen takes her place among those who quietly serve almost unnoticed in the background as others lead noisily in the spotlight. However, soon her indomitable spirit and remarkable strength are recognized as a steadying force in the group. Notice her perspective in the following comments. "[In stealth soul friendship] I mostly listen to someone else and pray through that. . . . I love to listen to others talking about what they got out of the reading assignments. . . . I loved the time in the paddle boat with my soul friend, sharing and hearing the heart of each of us. Precious time together." Her heart for her husband is touching in this remark, "I struggled with wondering if Ken was doing OK." Possibly, her resiliency comes from being a cancer survivor. Karen now ministers to women battling cancer. She also joyfully serves with the quilt makers at her church.

In spite of his natural shyness, Ken added tremendous value to the group by his humble transparency. He writes well, revealing a perceptive, analytical mind. As he gets used to retirement from the police force, Ken is learning to cherish his roles as a leader, a husband, father, and grandfather.

Rick is a dynamic speaker and always a forceful presence in the room. In his speech and in his writing, he uses creative flourishes, under-linings, upper case and exclamation points. He delivers powerful sermons in which the message is stated with clarity and passion. He and his wife, Carol, are transitioning from missions work in Brazil to the inner city of Portland, Oregon, where they will put their experience with the brokenness of poverty and addiction to good use. Rick is grateful for the tools he acquired through API, especially the soul friendship skills, which will stretch him spiritually to glorify God in ways that are new to him.

APPENDIX

We include this material as a testimony to the sustaining grace of God through a time of profound sorrow. During our nephew's three-year battle with brain cancer, our family drew deeply upon the Awakenings devotional pattern. The following is a testimony of strength in weakness shored up through numerous encounters with God through countless intercessions, breath prayer, lectio, and the deepest of soul friendships. Our prayer is that our experience will encourage other families who walk with Jesus through the valley of the shadow. The following is the message that I preached at Jeremy's memorial service on January 4, 2009.

– Pastor Wes Johnson

Jeremy Edward Johnson
Memorial Service
January 4, 2009

Before I begin my personal remarks, I would like to read a testimony from Alysha Abrams, Jeremy's wonderful sweetheart.

Jeremy's Memorial

Have you ever been so captivated by a sunset that you're at a loss for words? Stared at the glory and the colors so intertwined that it takes your breath away? That's what it was like for me every time I looked into Jeremy's eyes. Our love was something that most spend their whole lives searching for. He was my junior high sweetheart. It had to have been God ordained . . . it *had* to be divine intervention . . . there's just no other explanation for how two people could meet at twelve, lose contact around fourteen, reunite at nineteen, lose contact at twenty, then reunite at twenty-three and fall so madly in love. How could two people's paths keep crossing like that if it wasn't God? Jeremy was my rock; he showed me what strength is all about. He was my spiritual leader; taught me about faith. He was my warrior; he taught me about the battle of good and evil and how to prevail. He was my confidence when I had lost all of my own. He *is* my heart and the love of my life.

Cancer is ugly. It's a lie sent from the enemy to make us believe that life is over . . . but neither cancer nor death can take away *yesterday*. It can't take away all the things that Jeremy taught me. It can't take away all the memories we made. It can't take away his voice that will forever resound in my head. It can't take away the roses that he sent me, the dates we had, the cheap Chinese food he'd try to force me to eat or the many, *many* sunsets that we watched as he held me on the beach, and it can never erase the love that we share. It might stop the earthly wedding that we spoke of but *nothing* can stop us from spending eternity together. I'll meet you in heaven baby . . . and I'll *still* be wearing that white dress.

First of all, as a family we want to thank Pastor Barry Crane and the North Sound Church family for walking so closely with us through these last several months. My wife Kathryn and I have been in Gary and Linda's home repeatedly and eaten of the great food that you have dropped by. Some of you have cooked, some have cleaned, all you have prayed. Pastor Barry, we thank you for being with us, especially on the day Jeremy was born into eternity. Thank you for being a good and dedicated servant of the Lord. In addition, we are forever grateful for the skilled doctors, technicians, and the countless caregivers in the hospital and clinic. You have given us three precious years with our Jeremy. In his closing days, you wonderful hospice workers have given us a great gift in your love and skillful care.

And Sam Hirst, you spent many a night at Jeremy's bedside. God bless you for being Jeremy's friend all these years, training as a nurse and then giving of your skill to our family. His parents slept better knowing you were there.

And we want to thank Pastor Alec Rowland for his visits and his prayers with Jeremy during this battle. I am told that when Pastor Alec asked Jeremy, "What would you like us to pray for?" Jeremy replied, "I want to know God closer and deeper." What a wonderful request. Certainly Jeremy longed for God to heal him. But he also showed a seasoned wisdom in that request. His was like the Apostle Paul's request and desire expressed in Philippians:

> I want to know Christ—yes, to know the power of his resurrection and participation in his sufferings, becoming like him in his death, and so, somehow, attaining to the resurrection from the dead.
>
> —Phil. 3:10-11

God answered Jeremy's prayer, both in his life experience and in his birth into eternity. Now he gazes upon the face of Jesus. This has intensified our meditations on heaven. It is more real to us now. Jeremy is the first of our generations to cross over.

I want to say that we have grown to know God better through this ordeal. And that is our passion—that you know the Lord in a deep and rich way. That was Jeremy's passion. At one point he expressed this to Alysha:

> He looked at me one night (sometime in late October) and said, "I hope you don't plan on having much money, Babe. Missionary families usually don't make much." Then he smiled. . . . It was his goal to have his story told and to bring as many people to Christ as he possibly could. God seemed to have a different plan. Jeremy left this world on December 13 at 11:45 am. His father was on his left side, his mother, brother and myself on his right. I held his hand as he took his last breath and he ended his earthly walk peacefully. Although Jeremy is no longer here to tell his story, I would like to see his dream of saving souls through his powerful testimony fulfilled.

I once had a best friend ask me, "What is a relationship with God like?" Today I want to let you in on what it has been like for us to walk with God through this battle over the last three years. In the book of Job, Job lifts his complaint to God for all the suffering he was going through. God never answered his question. But beginning in chapter 38 of that book, God reveals himself in power to his disappointed servant. God's presence transforms Job's question into an amazed, overwhelmed stillness that filled his soul. Job is simply overwhelmed in the palpable presence of his Maker:

Then Job answered the LORD:
"I am unworthy—how can I reply to you?
I put my hand over my mouth.
I spoke once, but I have no answer—
twice, but I will say no more".

—Job 40:3–5

Today I want to let you in on the ways that our family has met God in this suffering. We have met God and we want you to know that He is great company! It is our hope that you too, will come to know and love and be satisfied in the God who has revealed himself in the Bible and in life in such rich and compelling ways.

Here is a Scripture that invites us to find refuge in the character of our great God:

The name of the Lord is a fortified tower;
the righteous run to it and are safe.

—Prov. 18:10

Over the last several years I have been researching and writing and praying and teaching on ancient methods of contemplative prayer. Contemplative prayer is all about getting silent before the Lord, as Job did, and responding in the depths of one's soul to the depths of God's revelation. When we read and contemplate Scripture, we discover God's sufficiency. We experience the power of his name at the point of our soul's deepest need, and over time we find God meeting that need.

Good Shepherd, Comfort Me

I think it was three or four months after Jeremy's first craniotomy that I asked him what he most needed from God. "I can't hear God," Jeremy said. No wonder. The shock of a horrific diagnosis. Two surgeries where they opened his skull and removed cancerous tumors. Then weeks of radiation. "I can't hear God." Who would have a bit of a soul left after that kind of trauma? Few among us would have our spirits still in tune with the Holy Spirit.

So we looked together at a list of God's names that reveal his character to us. I explained that God reveals himself in Scripture through his names so that we may know him better and understand what he is offering us. I asked him which name of the Lord told him that God excels at speaking with his people. Jeremy pondered the list and chose Good Shepherd. I asked him what he wanted the Good Shepherd to do for him. "I could use some comfort," he said. Next we surveyed some Scriptures where the Lord reveals himself as the Good Shepherd. Jeremy chose Psalm 23. We read it together, and as we did, I asked J which words of the psalm resonated with his need. And he spoke it out clear and focused:

> Even though I walk
> through the valley of the shadow of death,
> I will fear no evil,
> for you are with me;
> your rod and your staff,
> they comfort me.
>
> —Ps. 23:4 NASB

So his prayer became, "Good Shepherd, comfort me."

A few weeks later, I asked him how his prayer was going and if he could hear God. And he said in his understated way, that things were better. As I was preparing to give this talk, I asked Gary and Linda and Alysha if Jeremy ever spoke of Psalm 23 or his prayer from that psalm. Alysha thought for a moment and then said that he would often hand her a Bible and ask her to read that psalm, but he never told her why he liked it. Quiet waters run deep.

Good Shepherd, Walk With Us in This Suffering

Later at a prayer seminar, without consulting Jeremy, my brother Gary also chose the Good Shepherd name. He also chose Psalm 23 and the same phrase from that psalm. While he pondered what he needed most from the Good Shepherd, he had occasion to meditate on the famous picture of Christ walking with the two dejected disciples on the road to Emmaus. "That's what I need Jesus to do for us—walk with us." And so he prayed that the Good Shepherd would walk with them through this dark valley of the shadow. Both father and son were praying over the same holy words of God. And the Lord walked with us all through the valley.

Jeremy's brother Greg read us his poem just now about the attitude of courage that Jeremy showed during this three-year battle.

Courageous Warrior
by Greg Johnson

You walked a road that was overflowed with pain
When you heard the word that it was back again.
Your future seemed, as your tears streamed, to be lost,
Yet you resolved your heart to not fall apart, and the bridge of fear was crossed.

With head held high to the sunset sky you prayed
To hear God's voice and make the choice to let him have his way
Then armed with strength for the great length of the road
You journeyed towards the sound of death's chords and you showed

I'm never giving in to this hopelessness before me
I want to know God more and behold his glory
I am a courageous warrior, yes! That is my name
I walked the road with strength until the angels came.

Lion of Judah, Grant Us Your Courage

This was one of the prayers we relied upon when Jeremy first received his diagnosis.

I was meditating on Revelation 5 when I first developed this prayer. The chapter describes the incredible vision of the throne room of heaven that the Lord allowed John the beloved. The Father is seated on the throne in blinding glory. He holds in his hand the scroll that entitles only one person to take ownership of the earth and prepare it for the Lord to rule. But no one was found worthy.

John experienced deep grief until his attention was directed unto Jesus:

> I wept and wept because no one was found who was worthy to open the scroll or look inside. Then one of the elders said to me, "Do not weep! See, the Lion of the tribe of Judah, the Root of David, has triumphed. He is able to open the scroll and its seven seals." Then I saw a Lamb, looking as if it had been slain, standing at the center of the throne, encircled by the four living creatures and the elders.
>
> —Rev. 5:4-6

Jesus is the Lion who triumphs as a Lamb. He is victorious through weakness. Jesus evidenced an overwhelming courage as the Lion of Judah. Now we needed the deep courage that Jesus showed in going to the cross. And how did Jesus deal with the specter of his own death? He submitted himself to the Father's will in Gethsemane, suffered the injustice of men; he walked Calvary's mountain with courage, died with integrity of purpose, and rose triumphant on the third day. This is more than a Bible story; it is the path we all must tread. Our Savior has walked it ahead of us. He is our leader, our captain. I want to follow his path with the same courage. And so we had this prayer going through the battle; "Lion of Judah, grant us your courage." Jeremy reflected the courage of his Savior, who triumphed through his own suffering. I asked Gary and Linda about what they saw in Jeremy's courage. They said that during this battle, on countless trips to the hospital for tests, diagnosis, and grueling treatment, Jeremy walked through every door, very tall and strong and resolutely. He would ask, "What are we going to do next?" Instead of asking "Why me," he asked, "What's next?"

Jeremy had a strong will as a child. As a young boy he also seemed impervious to pain. That strong will served him well when he set his mind on this battle. "What else can I do?" he asked. Once he got clarity about the next step his attitude was: "This is what needs to be done." Even at his appointments in the hospital he would strut in, that famous heel-first—feet sideways kind of walk that he did—heels taking the lead almost—he would strut in and lead his mom or Alysha into the building. His attitude was, let's get 'er done. It's no wonder that a dear family friend had the trophy made with the inscription—*Jeremy Johnson, Courageous Warrior.*

When told that the cancer had spread to his spine and was all through his brain fluid, he was quiet; he did not show any outward sign of trauma. While others were weeping, Jeremy was quiet and still. He was chin up, calm, and quiet. King David wrote of that confidence that flows from the Lord:

> The LORD is my light and my salvation—
> whom shall I fear?
> The LORD is the stronghold of my life—
> of whom shall I be afraid?
> I am still confident of this:
> I will see the goodness of the LORD
> in the land of the living.
> Wait for the LORD;
> be strong and take heart
> and wait for the LORD.
>
> —Ps. 27:1, 13–14

Gary and Linda spoke of his staying power even as a boy. Alysha witnessed a whole new level of courage in him. She wrote about it on her blog.

> Jeremy's bravery was astonishing. After he got the news on September 10 and returned home, we lay on his bed and wept for the fear that our life together was going to end prematurely. After a short time he sat up and said, "I'm not going to do this. *We're* not going to do this! We're not going to sit here crying. We're not going to spend our time this way. We're going on a date!" That was his attitude over the remainder of his life. He was not going to feel bad for himself or let anyone pity him. He was determined to live every day that he had left with a positive attitude. He stated many times that, "The devil is a liar," and Jeremy never let fear or the devil's lies control his thoughts or emotions. He was brave, a gallant warrior.
> http://www.myspace.com/remember_jeremy

There was a moment in the hospital after his second craniotomy when Jeremy cruised into the waiting room on his wheelchair, guiding it with his feet. We were all sitting, sad and moping, and here he came in his hospital robe, smiling and happy to see us all. That's the way he traveled the entire three-year journey. Courage is a twin to encouragement. Courage lifts our spirits in the face of fear. Encouragement is shared courage. It is grace under fire. When incoming rounds are hitting and wounding those close to us, still we experienced that courageous warrior spirit.

After Jeremy's third craniotomy, Alysha had to reevaluate whether she could go the distance with the man that she loved. They had been buddies and friends and girlfriend boyfriend off and on since seventh grade. And in the middle of 2007, Alysha gave Gary and Linda a page out of her journal where she was writing of her fears. "Do I go for it and love him, or do I pull back?" She decided in that journal entry to overcome her fears and stick with Jeremy through his pain. She quoted the old phrase, "It is better to have loved and lost than not to have loved at all." Alysha, our family loves you and is so grateful for your courage in the fellowship of Jeremy's suffering.

That was another prayer our family had going through these three years.

Courage Is the Way to Lead

> For it was fitting for Him, for whom *are* all things and by whom *are* all things, in bringing many sons to glory, to make the captain of their salvation perfect through sufferings.
>
> —Heb. 2:10 NKJV

Jesus, the captain of our salvation, earned that title through the pains of his own death. He fulfilled the completeness of God's mission for him through the things he suffered. Think of the courage that Jesus demonstrated in the Garden of Gethsemane when he submitted to the Father's will. Jesus gathered up the fragments of his overwhelmed soul and marched resolutely forward. He was whipped viciously, beaten beyond recognition. And when he stumbled beneath that horrid cross, Simon of Cyrene shared in the fellowship of his sufferings. Simon carried that cross with Jesus, the blood of Christ smeared upon his strong shoulders as he lifted the heavy cross. What did it mean for Simon to share in the sufferings of Jesus? The Apostle Paul longed to share in this fellowship of suffering. Jeremy shared in this suffering with Jesus. And we who loved Jeremy and cared for him and prayed for him and changed his bandages and administered his medication, we also shared in the fellowship of Jeremy's suffering.

Early on, we told him, "You are our leader. You are the first among us to fight this battle. You are walking point. You are the first of our generations to lead the way through the valley of the shadow of death. All of us must go that way." And we told Jeremy repeatedly that he was our leader, and that we were there to support him and get him everything in our power to help him do the mission that was assigned to him. He was walking point in this battle, and we were there to support him in every way.

We were there to support Gary and Linda as they carried the weight of this war. How Gary and Linda did it is beyond me.

How did this Mom and Dad do it?
How did they serve . . .
 So resolute
 So focused
 So detailed?

How did they master
 The administration of numerous medications
 Long names, complicated dosing schedules
 Jeremy suffering long nights of
 Pain, nausea?

How did they find grace
to turn their son upon his bed of pain?

How did they speak
Like clinicians
    Of medical care
    And paralysis
    Through long and painful days?
And then weep as a father
Sorrow as a mother
    Seeing their strong, beautiful son
    Losing the use of his legs,

    Then his right hand,
    Then his strength failed
    And he could no longer lift his head from the pillow.

Gary led the way in the fellowship of this suffering.
Linda courageously attended to every detail.
Unrelenting mercy.
They shouldered the heavy pack
And carried it through deep winter snows
Up the steep trail.

Jeremy was our captain
Gary his chief servant
Linda his comforter.

Jeremy leading the way through Gates of Splendor
Gary leading the way of service,
Supporting his beloved son
In whom
He was well-pleased.

Gary and Linda, you served your son with honor. You respected his integrity, his judgments, his wishes. You laid down your lives for him, and we respect you and honor you and are proud to see the character of Jesus revealed in you. You have demonstrated the way of Christ and we are learning from you the way of courageous and sacrificial service.

Jeremy's suffering has a much greater meaning, because it was linked to the suffering of his courageous Savior. Jeremy relied on Jesus, the captain of his salvation. In this way the captain of our salvation earned the right to give life and salvation to those who would renounce their own efforts and ask him to come and be their leader, to lead them to the place where they cannot go on their own.

One other prayer rooted us in the character of God through our journey through the valley of the shadow of death.

Lamb of God, Triumph in Our Suffering

This was a second prayer that flowed out of Revelation, chapter 5. "Lord Jesus, get your triumph from our pain. Just as you triumphed through your own suffering and death, so now get your victory, your glory, through our pain. Make sure that whatever else happens, you get your triumph out of it."

Everything in us wanted to see Jeremy healed. We longed for a rich and full life with marriage, and children, and family reunions for the next generations. But this was not to be. So what we asked for from the beginning was that whatever happened, that Jesus would get what he wanted out of our pain. As long as he got his triumph, we would be okay. Yes, we would be torn and grieving. Yes, we would carry this wound for the rest of our lives. But this we share in common with all creation.

It became of great comfort to understand that in our suffering, the Spirit of God moans and aches. In our suffering, the Holy Spirit prays with groans too deep for words. In Romans 8, the Apostle Paul wrote of the ache in creation and the blessing of the new creation sustaining God's people through suffering:

> I consider that our present sufferings are not worth comparing with the glory that will be revealed in us. The creation waits in eager expectation for the sons of God to be revealed. For the creation was subjected to frustration, not by its own choice, but by the will of the one who subjected it, in hope that the creation itself will be liberated from its bondage to decay and brought into the glorious freedom of the children of God.

We know that the whole creation has been groaning as in the pains of childbirth right up to the present time. Not only so, but we ourselves, who have the firstfruits of the Spirit, groan inwardly as we wait eagerly for our adoption as sons, the redemption of our bodies. For in this hope we were saved. But hope that is seen is no hope at all. Who hopes for what he already has? But if we hope for what we do not yet have, we wait for it patiently.

In the same way, the Spirit helps us in our weakness. We do not know what we ought to pray for, but the Spirit himself intercedes for us with groans that words cannot express. And he who searches our hearts knows the mind of the Spirit, because the Spirit intercedes for the saints in accordance with God's will.

—Rom. 8:18–27 emphasis mine

At the risk of sounding like a pastoral theologian, (now, why would I sound like that?) let me tell you how I have been processing our situation in light of this amazing passage. Because of Adam's fall, God has subjected all of creation to futility; it is all decaying. In the case of our mom, cancer that was cured in 1997 returned in 2008. In the case of our dad, his summer remission from pancreatic cancer was short lived. Jeremy had eight months cancer free. And then it returned with a vengeance. Creation is subject to such futility. But this suffering is not just zeroing in on us, as though something unusual were happening to us. All of creation groans. We are part of a fallen creation. So we Johnsons are aching and groaning right along with the rest of the planet. Our loved ones are suffering decay, as generations have through the ages. We pray for God's miraculous intervention, but are aware that to intervene in a miraculous way God would be putting a huge reversal on the results of Adam's fall. Someday all creation will be liberated from this decay, but maybe not right now.

But I have to tell you that as the old creation falls apart, the New Creation is active now in our lives. The Holy Spirit is so precious! So right now, the Holy Spirit aches deep within us; he communes with the Father and prays for us according to the Father's will. And what is the Father's will? We want healing; but God wants living reflections of his Son. The Holy Spirit is all about the business of forming us to take on the character and mission of Jesus (Rom. 8:29).

Jeremy received Jesus as Savior when he was a young boy. Through this battle with cancer, Jeremy gained a deeper and closer knowledge, a first-hand experience with almighty God. Jeremy chose to draw close to his leader, Jesus. He attached his faith to his captain's lead and followed on with courage. We need that courage now. Jeremy triumphed through his suffering. You and I can triumph if we will entrust our souls to our Creator, if we will turn our wills over to the Savior who triumphed through his own suffering. Come to the Savior. Turn your life and your death over to him.

I love this beautiful prayer by Philip Newell. It is published in his devotional, *Celtic Benediction*.

> As it was in the stillness of the morning
> So may it be in the silence of the night.
> As it was in the hidden vitality of the womb
> So may it be at my birth into eternity.
> As it was in the beginning, O God,
> So in the end may of your gift be born
> So in the end may your gift of life be born.

So may your end be—contemplated with hope in the Lord who brought you into this world. Seek the Lord while he may be found, call on him while he is near. Let the wicked forsake his way, and let him turn to the Lord and be saved.

Dr. Wes Johnson, Jeremy's uncle

BIBLIOGRAPHY

Anderson, Keith, and Randy D. Reese. *Spiritual Mentoring: A Guide for Seeking and Giving Direction.* Downers Grove, IL: InterVarsity Press, 1999.

Arthur, Kay. *Lord I Want To Know You: A Devotional Study on the Names of God.* Colorado Springs, CO: Waterbrook Press, 1992.

Bakke, Jeannette A. *Holy Invitations: Exploring Spiritual Direction.* Grand Rapids, MI: Baker Books, 2000.

Card, Michael. *A Sacred Sorrow Experience Guide: Reaching out to God in the Lost Language of Lament.* 1st ed. Colorado Springs, CO: NavPress, 2005.

Cawsey, T. F., and Gene Deszca. *Toolkit for Organizational Change.* Los Angeles, CA: Sage Publications, 2007.

Dow, Philip E. *Virtuous Minds: Intellectual Character Development.* Downers Grove, Illinois: IVP Academic, 2013.

Foster, Richard J. *Prayer: Finding the Heart's True Home.* 1st ed. San Francisco, CA: HarperSanFrancisco, 1992.

Fuqua, Dennis. *Living Prayer: The Lord's Prayer Alive In You.* Sisters, OR: Deep River Books, 2012.

Giardini, Fabio. *Pray Without Ceasing: Toward a Systematic Psychotheology of Christian Prayer life.* Leominster, UK: Gracewing, 1998

Johnson, Jan. *When the Soul Listens: Finding Rest and Direction in Contemplative Prayer.* Colorado Springs, CO: NavPress, 1999.

Johnson, Wesley E. *Morning, Noon and Night, a Trinitarian Devotional.* Everett, WA: Awakenings Prayer Institute, www. AwakeningsPrayerInstitute.org, 2015.

Jones, Cheslyn, Geoffrey Wainwright, and Edward Yarnold. *The Study of Spirituality.* New York, NY: Oxford University Press, 1986.

Laubach, Frank C. *Letters by a Modern Mystic: Excerpts from Letters Written to his Father.* Colorado Springs, CO: Purposeful Design Publications, 2007.

Lewis, C. S. *The Problem of Pain.* San Francisco, CA: HarperSanFrancisco, 2001.

Mulholland, M. Robert. *Shaped by the Word: The Power of Scripture in Spiritual Formation.* Nashville, TN: Upper Room, 1985.

Newell, J. Philip. *Celtic Benediction: Morning and Night Prayer.* Grand Rapids, MI: William B. Eerdmans Pub. Co., 2000.

Oehler, Gustaf, and George Edward Day. *Theology of the Old Testament.* 8th ed. New York and London: Funk & Wagnalls company, 1883.

Wiersbe, Warren. *Be Loyal: Following the King of Kings.* Colorado Springs, CO: David C. Cook, 2008.

INDEX

SCRIPTURE INDEX

ENDNOTES

Introduction

1. C. S. Lewis, *The Problem of Pain*, (San Francisco, CA: HarperSanFrancisco, 2001), 93.

Chapter 1

2. Words of hope and their explanations shared on retreat. Used by permission.

Chapter 2

3. Richard J. Foster, *Prayer: Finding the Heart's True Home*, 1st ed. (San Francisco, CA: HarperSanFrancisco, 1992), 155.
4. J. Philip Newell, *Celtic Benediction: Morning and Night Prayer* (Grand Rapids, MI.: William B. Eerdmans Pub. Co., 2000). This little book of devotions is beautifully illustrated with Seventh Century Celtic drawings.

Chapter 3

5. Philip E. Dow, *Virtuous Minds: Intellectual Character Development*. (Downers Grove, Illinois: IVP Academic, 2013).

6. Foster, 144–145.
7. M. Robert Mulholland, *Shaped by the Word: The Power of Scripture in Spiritual Formation* (Nashville, TN: Upper Room, 1985).
8. Author's recollection of exegesis class notes at Dallas Seminary.
9. Foster, 144.
10. Foster, 146.
11. Cheslyn Jones, Geoffrey Wainwright, and Edward Yarnold, *The Study of Spirituality* (New York, NY: Oxford University Press, 1986), 333.
12. Ibid.
13. Ibid.
14. Edith related this story to us at Thanksgiving that year. Later, I asked Karen about it, and she confirmed it as true.
15. Foster, 142.
16. Michael Card, *A Sacred Sorrow: Reaching out to God in the Lost Language of Lament*, 1st ed. (Colorado Springs, CO: NavPress, 2005).
17. Dennis Fuqua, *Living Prayer: The Lord's Prayer Alive in You,* (Sisters, Oregon: Deep River Books, 2012).
18. Jan Johnson, *When the Soul Listens: Finding Rest and Direction in Contemplative* Prayer (Colorado Springs, CO: NavPress, 1999).

Chapter 4

19. Mulholland, 126.
20. Thomas Keating, 2006. http://www.thecentering.org/centering_method.html, accessed July 21, 2015.
21. Luke 1:38, author's paraphrase.
22. Keating 2006 http://www.centeringprayer.com/lectio_divina.html.
23. Walter Bennis quoted in T. F. Cawsey and Gene Deszca, *Toolkit for Organizational Change* (Los Angeles, CA: Sage Publications, 2007), 251.

24. Theresa Schaudies 2014, Reflecting on Reflection, http://www.awakeningsprayer.org/reflecting-on-reflection/. Posted November 12, 2014.
25. Wesley E. Johnson, *Morning, Noon, and Night, a Trinitarian Devotional*, (available at www.AwakeningsPrayer.org.)
26. Cited by Dicken from *Night*, I i.2, in Jones, Wainwright, and Yarnold, 371.
27. Ibid., 372.
28. Ibid.

Chapter 5

29. Warren Wiersbe, *Be Loyal: Following the King of Kings*, (Colorado Springs, David C. Cook, 2008), 103.
30. Gustav Frederich Oehler and George Edward Day, *Theology of the Old Testament*, 8th ed. (New York and London,: Funk & Wagnalls company, 1883), 125.
31. Foster, 134.
32. Tsichlis 2006 http://www.goarch.org/en/ourfaith/articles/article7104.asp
33. Ibid.
34. This was edited and expanded by Wes Johnson from "The Names of God" by J. Hampton Keathley, III , Th.M. *http://www.bible.org/page.asp?page_id=220*. For additional resources on breath prayer development, visit www.awakeningsprayer.com.

Chapter 6

35. Fabio Giardini, *Pray Without Ceasing: Toward a Systematic Psychotheology of Christian Prayer Life*, (Leominster, Gracewing, 1998), 387.
36. Ibid.
37. For further discussion of how God forms a leader throughout a lifetime, see Terry Walling, *Focusing Leaders Participants' Manual*, (Church Resource Ministries, 1993).
38. Ibid.

39. Frank C. Laubach, *Letters from a Modern Mystic,* (Colorado Springs, CO: Purposeful Design Publications, 2007).

Chapter 7

40. Ted Chamberlain, *National Geographic News,* http://news.nationalgeographic.com/news/2006/06/060613-cat-bear.html.
41. Sampson Brueher's song, *He Will Carry Me,* was among the most-performed songs of 2005. *He Will Carry Me* written by Sampson Brueher, Dennis Kurttila and Mark Schultz; Publishers Be Together Music, Crazy Romaine Music and Kurttila Songs, http://www.rctimes.com/apps/pbcs.dll/article?AID=/20060404/ENTERTAINMENT01/604040358/1005/MTCN0303.
42. C.S. Lewis, "As the Ruin Falls" http://www.poemhunter.com/poem/as-the-ruin-falls-2/ , accessed July 2015.
43. Phil Keaggy, recorded on *Love Broke Through,* October 1976 http://www.philkeaggy.com/discography-1/
44. *C. S. Lewis, The Problem of Pain: The Intellectual Problem Raised by Human Suffering Examined with Sympathy and Realism.* (New York: Macmillan, 1976), 93.

Chapter 8

45. Ibid.
46. Kay Arthur, *Lord I Want To Know You: A Devotional Study on the Names of God.* (Colorado Springs, CO: Waterbrook Press, 1992).

Chapter 9

47. In the Awakenings Prayer Institute, we devote considerable time to training for this vital role.
48. Jeannette A. Bakke, *Holy Invitations: Exploring Spiritual Direction,* (Grand Rapids, MI: Baker Books) 43.
49. Bakke, 25.

50. Keith Anderson and Randy D. Reese, *Spiritual Mentoring: A Guide for Seeking and Giving Direction* (Downers Grove, IL: InterVarsity Press, 1999), 44.
51. Ibid., 42.
52. Ibid., 95.
53. Bakke, 102.
54. Bakke, 95.

Contact Information

To order additional copies of this book, please visit
www.redemption-press.com.
Also available on Amazon.com and BarnesandNoble.com
Or by calling toll free 1-844-2REDEEM.

CPSIA information can be obtained
at www.ICGtesting.com
Printed in the USA
FSOW01n0447160317
31753FS